The Essential Daughter

Changing Expectations for Girls at Home, 1797 to the Present

Mary Collins

PRAEGER

Westport, Connecticut
London

Library of Congress Cataloging-in-Publication Data

Collins, Mary, 1961–
    The essential daughter : changing expectations for girls at home, 1797 to
the present / Mary Collins.
      p. cm.
    Includes bibliographical references and index.
    ISBN 0-275-97836-2 (alk. paper)
    1. Women—United States—Family relationships—History. 2. Daughters—
United States—Biography. 3. Sex role—United States. I. Title.
HQ1410.C59 2002
306.874'0973—dc21   2002072538

British Library Cataloguing in Publication Data is available.

Library of Congress Catalog Card Number: 2002072538
ISBN: 0-275-97836-2

First published in 2002

Praeger Publishers, 88 Post Road West, Westport, CT 06881
An imprint of Greenwood Publishing Group, Inc.
www.praeger.com

Printed in the United States of America

The paper used in this book complies with the
Permanent Paper Standard issued by the National
Information Standards Organization (Z39.48–1984).

10 9 8 7 6 5 4 3 2 1

The author and publisher gratefully acknowledge permission to quote from the
following sources: Betty Friedan Papers, Schlesinger Library, Radcliffe Institute, Harvard University. Adrietta Applegate Hixon, *On to Oregon* (Fairfield, WA:
Ye Galleon Press). Permission kindly granted by Ye Galleon Press. Excerpts
from *The Spencers of Amberson Avenue: A Turn-of-the-Century Memoir*, by Ethel
Spencer, edited by Michael P. Weber and Peter N. Stearns, © 1983, 1984.
Reprinted by permission of the University of Pittsburgh Press. Every reasonable
effort has been made to trace the owners of copyrighted materials in this book,
but in some instances this has proven impossible. The author and publisher will
be glad to receive information leading to more complete acknowledgments in
subsequent printings of the book and in the meantime extend their apologies
for any omissions.

For Julia

CONTENTS

Photographic essay follows page 84.

PREFACE

Back in the 1970s and 1980s, when I used to play a lot of basketball on public courts, I always felt the most important thing I did every week was to insert myself in the all-male games at my local recreation center. As a former college player I had the skill to play with most of the men and I knew it. I took every opportunity I could to make sure they knew it too. Often, when a crowd at a particular gym had finally accepted me as a first-class player, I'd purposely move to another court, just so I could make the point again. I have always been somewhat belligerent about asserting my equality.

So how did I—a former college athlete, one-time single parent, and working mom—come to write a book that claims girls need a more fulfilling role at home? Like every self-respecting professional woman, I am painfully aware of the oppressive patterns of the past and for years I have fought every stereotype. But when I set out to write a history of girlhood in America, I was struck by how many of the girls' personal accounts from the eighteenth, nineteenth, and early twentieth centuries sang with a self-confidence that we are hard-pressed to instill in our own daughters today. No, they did not have the educational or career opportunities of their brothers, and that was awful, but they clearly gained something from having a vital role in their household economies. The historical record speaks for itself.

While I would never advocate that we return to a damaging and sexist division of labors, in which the girls get stuck at home and the boys go on to excel in sports, education, and careers, I do believe we need to rethink the blank slate that was left behind when we turned our back on old domestic patterns. Nothing that we have to offer our children in their public lives can replace what they once gained from playing an essential role within their families. In my research I have found this to be true for both boys and girls, but because each sex has had such a different domestic history, I felt I could only address one part of the problem in this book. Resurrecting a vibrant private role for daughters is the more difficult dilemma. If we can have a candid dialogue about that, a more balanced role for sons will emerge as well.

After some extensive reading, I began my serious archival research at Radcliffe College in Cambridge, Massachusetts, where the Schlesinger Library has a large collection of women's papers. I came armed with my black-and-white mind-set, certain that the girls who lived in Boston in the 1790s or in Lowell during the Industrial Revolution must have been downtrodden and practically illiterate. Their lack of education and opportunities must have made them miserable. Instead I found elegant accounts that had a lilt about them that I hope I can instill in my own daughter as she matures.

Lucy Larcom hated working in the mills, but she loved being useful to her family. Lizzie Perkins longed to travel to all of the strange places her father had been, but she also took great pride in serving as the lead hostess of the household when her mother became ill. These girls, and many of the others I profile, felt loved, needed, skilled, even, on a certain level, important. I confess I did not want to see these positive strands. I did not want to admit that past domestic patterns might actually have something positive to offer us if we would only sort through the chaff.

But after reading Mary Ellen Todd's account of her journey West, I knew I was on to something if I could just open my mind enough to accept it. There she was just a nine-year-old girl caring for her ailing father, pregnant mother, two baby sisters, and all of the livestock for several days during one awful stretch of their journey. "I tell you, those were bad times, requiring courage to keep up and going," she told her grandchildren years later. Battling back a sense of panic, Mary Ellen, and her sixteen-year-old adopted brother John, greased wheels, found good grass for the livestock, built fires, and cooked meals.

As her parents regained their strength, she returned to her role as mother's helper with relief. Now someone else could take charge. But with each stride across the prairie and with each challenge successfully met, Mary Ellen's concept of what it meant to be a girl expanded. By the time the family settled into their new cabin in Happy Valley, Oregon, Mary Ellen had become expert at cracking her father's great bullwhip, something her mother considered quite unladylike. But Mary Ellen relished the idea of having the "power to set things going" and saw that power in herself.

Even with this kind of evidence staring me in the face, it took me three years to summon the courage to admit that many parents from the nineteenth century raised sturdier, more confident daughters. The current trend toward measuring self-worth in public arenas—sports contests and test taking are just two examples—has left us with a large population of shaky, self-absorbed children. We must work on their private lives if we hope to counteract some of the more persistent societal problems: teen pregnancy, drug use, eating disorders, and more. This book argues that Americans must reassess the role of *all* family members if they hope to build a domestic life for a girl that makes her feel wanted, skilled, and relevant no matter how well she performs on the field or in the classroom. It is time to face the fact that girls need a clearer role at home, and it does not have to come at the expense of all of the other gains we have made for them.

When I look back on my own childhood, I know I first felt essential to my family when my father died. Like most middle-class girls in the 1970s, I was allowed to expend the bulk of my energy on playful activities, such as basketball games; but then the cancer set in and took my dad within months. He was fifty-six; I was fourteen.

I remember lugging clothes downstairs to the car. My legs trembled from the work because I had worn myself out earlier in the day running quarter miles as part of my high school track practice. The relentless repetition and pain seemed a fitting metaphor for my inner emotional pace.

We were moving, because the memories hung too thick in the house for my mother to stand it anymore.

"What are you doing?" she snapped, as she spied me resting. "Tricia and you need to bring all those shirts downstairs."

"Mom, I'm so tired," I said.

"We're all tired," she added, and walked inside.

I began to cry, thinking it so unfair that I was expected to do anything after the hard practice I had endured. I was a founder of the team and one of the best sprinters in New England. Why were we leaving the last place my dad had been with us, anyway?

My mother came outside, the sunlight gone now, and barked at me again. Something in the way she stood, like a faint imprint of what she was before my father died, made me realize for the first time that she could not do it all by herself. My older sister, Tricia, and I had to find the physical strength to help her. I went inside, still crying, but more from the exhaustion and the knowing than anything else. We worked several more hours that evening. I do not recall if we stopped for dinner.

Something shifted in me that day I helped my mother move. Up to that point, I had felt something of a burden to her. As the youngest of four, I knew she worried about me the most. Her neediness in the gloaming of that day actually softened the sense I had of myself as a weight upon her. She needed my help and, to my surprise, I had something to give.

My brother, a graduate student at Columbia University in New York, began saving from his meager earnings in case of an "emergency," he said. Now, as an adult, I know the $500 or so he managed to squirrel away did not amount to much, but it was his mind-set that mattered. We all had to participate in "raising" and sustaining the family now. My older sister Betty transferred from Mount Holyoke College in South Hadley, Massachusetts, to Trinity College in Hartford, Connecticut, my hometown, so she could be closer to the family. The two of us still left at home became much more conscious of doing chores and earning spare change baby-sitting or delivering papers.

I continued to train intensely and won enough games and races to make a name for myself. My junior year I went to the Junior Olympic tryouts for basketball. But I knew I could no longer afford to put myself and my athletic skill at the center of things. If I came home exhausted from working out, I tried now to show it. I wanted my mother to think I had plenty of physical energy left over to help. Nothing I did on the court or track was as important as doing the dishes for my exhausted parent.

Later, as an adult raising a daughter on my own, I experienced the same intense level of dependency. With no father, and extended family more than an hour away, Julia learned early that she and I had to help each other. She sensed my exhaustion at the end of the day after working, cooking, and cleaning. She would race around picking up toys or ask to help set the table; anything to dispel the sense that she could not contribute in some small way. And I encouraged her can-do spirit even though she was only three.

One evening while eating dinner she announced that she wanted to run away with one of her best friends from preschool. "But Julia," I asked, half jokingly, "who would set the table for me?" A serious look settled over her face, followed by a silence.

"Mom," she said, "I'd come home each night and set the table for you, then I'd go see my friend." It never crossed her mind that I could do it without her.

As my Julia grows, I continue to worry about how I can help her sustain her sense of self-importance and confidence. I look around me at girls who have entered their middle-school years, and the view from my suburban seat outside of Washington, D.C., is not very good. So many of them log countless hours in front of televisions and computers. Those who do get involved in things such as soccer just seem to be passing the time. Except for the most gifted among them, sports have become just another way to "keep busy."

Few of the contemporary girls I interviewed for this book had any regular chores at home. Almost none of them garden, sew, do dishes, or any other group family activities that were so bonding for past generations. One of them even told me that her parents just did not want to be hassled with showing her how to clean a toilet properly or scrub the pans left from dinner, so she did nothing around the house. Nothing.

Sociological studies show that sons help out even less than daughters. While girls may pitch in as much as ten hours a week when they have two full-time working parents, boys rarely contribute more than three.[1] Domestic work is no longer part of some larger family dynamic for survival. It has become something no one wants to do, which means whoever is left holding the laundry bag is going to be hard-pressed to feel proud about that. So sexist attitudes and jaded views about housework in general have taken all the glitter off girls' contributions at home.

As Joan Brumberg notes in her big-selling book *The Body Project*, many girls fill the void opening within themselves by shopping for clothes and obsessing in general about how they look. The less essential they feel in the outside would, the more inward and self-absorbed they become. The process starts to work like a black hole, with the gravity of their inward stare finally pulling them under.

Countering such trends is going to involve hard work on a lot of fronts. The domestic front is a particularly dicey arena because past patterns have made most of us so gun-shy. I admit that sometimes while researching I would cry when I read about the smart girl who had to watch as her dull male cousin went off to college, or about the eleven-year-old who had to leave the classroom to work ten- to twelve-hour days in the mill. But—and I must keep returning to this qualifying word—other times I marveled at how many concrete skills these girls learned at such early ages: not just sewing and knitting, but also canning, handling stock, and working in the family fields.

I also noticed that many of the girls lost a sibling or parent before they reached adulthood. While I was unique among my peers to have my father die so young, I would not have been unique among past generations. Such losses just made those that were left all that more important to the survival of the family unit. The longer the youngest children remained dependent the more they imperiled the others. Kids of all ages quickly found a way to make themselves necessary. Being needed can be exhausting, but it is also empowering.

I have concluded that feeling essential to one's family is a vital part of growing up, a stage of development that many of today's daughters miss out on. The switch from dependent to contributor can be a lonely transition because you find yourself swinging in some middle ground between needing a parent and being needed. But one of the proudest days of my life remains the day I packed that car.

ACKNOWLEDGMENTS

This book was a deeply personal project that I did largely on my own, but certain people helped me in crucial ways, in particular Connie Collins Cain, Lynne Lamberg, Virginia Steffensen, Susan Tejada, and Robert Garnett, who all provided valuable editorial suggestions and much-needed encouragement following a terrible bike accident I had that almost derailed my girlhood project. My students and professional colleagues at Johns Hopkins University also inspired me with their own passion for their work. Every time I felt particularly bleak about the progress of this project, I would engage in a class discussion on writing that would get me thinking and hoping again.

I thank my husband, Andrew Macdonald, and our daughter, Julia, who put up with my writing binges, and my mother, sisters, and brother, who have always made me feel so positive about being a writer, an impractical profession at best. Finally, I wish to acknowledge my father, James Francis Collins, who managed to instill in me a love for history even though he died in 1975 when I was fourteen.

INTRODUCTION
No More Churning, Stitching, Kneading

The verbs have changed. American girls ages six to fourteen, who once spent their youthful energy churning, stitching, and kneading, now spend hours at the computer or on the soccer field. They do not have to weed and haul because girlish energy is no longer an essential commodity for the survival of the average American family. The idea that a contemporary Mollie, Connie, or Ally would skip school to do farm work or sewing seems as dated as the petticoat.

But something vital was also thrown out with all that drudgery: a family dynamic that made girls feel essential. In many early American homes parents needed their daughters to carry water, care for babies, weed gardens, sew, cook, and clean. Girlhood journals from these two centuries brim with stories of how they had to "take full charge of everything," because their mother had died or become too ill to work. A remarkable number of these girls felt proud of their contributions and loved their families and their place in them.

Before any of us can feel comfortable about what was positive about past domestic patterns, we must first face head-on the things that make us wince. Obviously there is a fine line between pitching in and being exploited. Many a struggling family in America forced their children into brutal work conditions for the sake of a few extra dollars a month. When Lucy Larcom's father died in 1831, her family put her to work in one of the textile mills in Lowell, Massachusetts, where she replaced bobbins ten hours a day for a dollar fifty a week. "The mill had its lessons for us. But it was not, and could not, be the right sort of life for a child," she wrote of her years among the machines.[1] Unfortunately, Lucy's mother needed her eleven-year-old daughter in the fiercest sense of the word, and what was right took a backseat to what was necessary.

By the turn of the twentieth century, American industry employed more than two million children under the age of sixteen. Immigrant girls, working in back rooms of tenement houses, pieced together artificial flowers or doll clothes for hours at a time. Boys sorted slate from coal in mines where the air turned their faces and lungs black. Both sexes worked as shrimp pickers, oyster shuckers, cotton pickers, and field hands.[2]

It is this dark side of neediness that led crusaders such as Jane Addams, founder of the Hull House in Chicago, and Lewis Hine, a photographer for the National Child Labor Committee, to battle the abusive work culture of American industry. They wrote about or took pictures of Manuel, the five-year-old shrimp picker, or Rosey, the seven-year-old oyster shucker. Stunning images of these child workers began springing up in newspapers and at lectures across the country. In the end, it was not their shabby clothes or dirty faces that disturbed people as much as their adult eyes. A five-year-old with a man's eyes.[3]

Today we look back in horror and wonder how adults at the time could have been accomplices to such a corrupt work culture. But really it was just an extreme example of the underlying ethic of usefulness that permeated American society. Asa Candler, one of the founders of Coca-Cola, put it bluntly when he said, "The most beautiful sight that we see is the child at labor. As early as he may get at labor the more beautiful and useful does his life get to be."[4]

The same extreme mind-set that allowed a black market in child workers often surfaced on the home front as well. Many families in small, rural towns felt girlhood was nothing more than a training ground for life as a housewife. After all, by the time they were ten, most girls had learned all that their parents felt they needed to know: cook, clean, sew, care for babies, and master letters well enough to read the Bible. Thus, many daughters seemed enslaved by their domestic obligations. They may have felt essential but rarely personally fulfilled and, perhaps, even overwhelmed.

Things did improve by World War I. Congress passed several child labor laws, and even though the courts kept knocking them down as unconstitutional, the legislation reflected a fundamental shift in public opinion. Eventually people such as Jane Addams began pushing states to enforce their school attendance laws, which required all children under the age of sixteen to attend school.[5]

Until that time very few people took girls' education seriously, and it would be many more decades before daughters achieved anything close to equality in the classrooms. In eighteenth-century America the idea of personal choice and a formal education simply did not exist for a girl. *A Vindication of the Rights of Woman,* in which author Mary Wollstonecraft argued that boys and girls be given the same liberal arts education,[6] had begun circulating in Boston and Philadelphia as early as 1792, but it was many years before substantive changes were made in the schools (1).

Of course, in a society in which practicality ruled, not even that many men had a higher education. In 1770 only three thousand citizens in the colonies had a college education (2). Obviously those numbers began to rise much more quickly for men than for women. Most charts do not even list the number of women in college prior to 1870 and even in that year less than one percent of the girls aged eighteen to twenty-one were enrolled in a four-year program (62). Not a very impressive record and certainly nothing that anyone should aspire to return to.

But all of these horrid tales overshadow a very important fact: Something in that culture of usefulness is worth salvaging. Those who felt needed in a positive, loving way, like Mary Ellen Todd as she walked to Oregon with her family, present a portrait of girlhood in eighteenth- and nineteenth-century America that is worth borrowing from.

As the labor-intensive life gave way to a world where the family could buy rather than make many of the things it needed, a girl's role within the home just swung to another extreme. Instead of taking part in the family economy, she was pushed completely outside of it. She became something that needed to be supported and protected, not included.

Instead of feeding livestock or contributing wages to her family, Mollie Gregory, a young girl who grew up in Alexandria, Virginia, during the Civil War, spent her days playing with dolls in the side garden or reading. "I was left pretty much to my own resources," she wrote in a journal. "War and rumors of war were nothing to nice little girls." The stench from the Union army's slaughterhouse, which stood just blocks away, must have filled her hideaway. She couldn't have missed the rows and rows of war prisoners laid out in the nearby field with no tents to protect them. And yet she did what her parents expected of her and turned her eyes from such unseemly things so she could focus on being a quiet, proper young lady, who would grow up to be a quiet, proper young wife.[7]

By the 1920s, all of these sheltered, economically useless daughters did begin to benefit from their newfound freedom because opportunities outside the home continued to expand for them. In 1900 there was just one women's college in America; by 1925 there were dozens. While many of them were nothing more than pricey finishing schools, a substantial number did have rigorous curriculums.[8] A girl who did well in high school could aspire to something more than just tutoring her future children. She could have a field of study that she explored for her own benefit, and, in rare instances, it led to a career.

The Depression forced families back into a survival mode and a girl's life contracted with it. Plenty of stores sold manufactured goods, but in the 1930s few families could afford them. One out of four adult men had no source of income.[9] Hand-sewn clothes, home-canned foods, and large vegetable gardens all became a regular part of family life again. That meant that lots of girls found themselves expending energy on chores instead of schoolwork or other outside activities.

Connie Sullivan, the second oldest child in a family of nine that lived in Pawtucket, Rhode Island, during the Depression, remembers that "when mother wasn't feeling well—she was carrying a child—she would keep Shirley and I home to iron. It took a whole day to iron for the family. I remember one day I really wanted to go to school—I was playing on the badminton team—but I had to stay home. Mother was so good, loved us so, worked so hard, you just helped—never complained."[10] The Sullivans could not afford to have Connie expend her precious energy on a sporting event that day. At various points, there were as many as thirteen people in the small one-floor house, all in need of food, clean clothes, and a place to sleep.

Despite such hardships, the idea that a girl could aspire to decent work outside the home, and even a college education, remained part of the new American social fabric. When the economy improved after World War II, families began pushing their girls outward again. The ultimate goal remained a good marriage, but there was a lot more a girl could do along the way.

By the 1950s and 1960s, most parents had placed their daughters firmly outside the family work flow. A girl's duty became increasingly linked with what she achieved outside the home and how that reflected on the family. The idea that a ten- or eleven-year-old would contribute vital cash to the household budget or do four or five hours of chores each day had become obsolete.

When Congress passed Title IX in 1972, it became illegal for school athletic programs to provide better equipment and coaches to boys' teams than to girls' teams. And while actual equality remains elusive, the law has pushed thousands of sports programs to encourage and train young girls. This tremendous shift has fed into the larger trend of having children focus their energies outside the home on things that boost their self-esteem.

A Lucy or Mary Ellen living today spends most of her "responsible" time doing homework, perfecting her standardize test-taking skills, and mastering extracurricular activities like soccer. She is most certainly not spending an entire day home from school to iron. The gains have been incremental; biases persist. But the underlying idea that girls have a future that includes much more than marriage and domestic chores has finally become firmly rooted in the American psyche.

But somehow all these splendid gains outside the home have not led to a culture full of confident young girls. Authors such as Joan Brumberg and Mary Pipher believe girlhood is now something of an "endangered species" threatened by all kinds of biological and social forces. As Brumberg illustrates in *The Body Project*, girls today not only menstruate sooner and have sex earlier than past generations but they also obsess more about their looks. The "character" projects, community projects, and family projects that once took up the time of most eighteenth- and nineteenth-century daughters have given way to simply "the body project."[11] Since the concept of beauty is a moving target, the chances for "success" remain elusive—the end result: dramatic problems with self-esteem among an alarmingly large number of young girls.

Back in the 1980s, Pipher, a psychiatrist in a midwestern town, began noticing a significant rise in the number of young teen girls coming to her because they mutilated themselves, battled drug or alcohol addictions, or had eating disorders. Equally disturbing, many of these patients were much younger than those Pipher normally saw for such problems. Listening to eleven-year-olds battle with bulimia sent Pipher out looking for some answers, which she wrote up in her best-selling book *Reviving Ophelia*.[12]

In the end Brumberg and Pipher concluded that America has become a society with a girl-poisoning culture. The media bombards them with too much sex and violence at too early an age. Working parents have less time to be around to offer an alternative view. Physically, modern girls develop at a much younger age than their grandmothers did but lack the nurturing, protective extended social network—like sewing circles—that Brumberg explains were such a vital shield for growing daughters in the nineteenth century.[13]

Calls for change remain abstract and outward looking: build a stronger sense of community, fight addiction, reform schools, curtail violence, promote gender equality. These are all laudable aims, but when measured against the day-to-day grind of life, they seem remote solutions at best.

Brumberg does recount the dramatic shift that took place around the Civil War in household economies: "Adolescent girls were not as essential as they had been before the war, when they were still needed to tend younger siblings and assist in household manufacturing." In the 1870s and 1880s, in particular, Americans saw a marked increase in goods produced outside the home, which of course freed up many a young hand. A national crisis ensued over the issue of what girls should do (6).

But neither Brumberg nor any other author writing for the main-stream, has explored what the loss of the household role has done to girls' self-esteem or what great potential such a hands-on and control-lable aspect of everyday life has for offering some solutions to the cri-sis among American daughters. In journal after journal stashed away in archives around the country, girls from the eighteenth and nine-teenth century speak with pride of how they helped their mothers every harvest season can vegetables that were vital to the family's winter diet. In some instances sixty or seventy years passed between the actual events and when the women wrote down their girlhood recollections, and yet it is these group activities—canning, gardening, washing—that they remember as crucial stages in their growing-up process. Today, girls are more apt to look back and remember hours on the soccer fields or basketball courts. Valuable "free" time for busy families now gets chewed up by the extracurricular craze.

Sports that used to be offered at school now run through local coun-ties, which means parents must ferry their kids to different fields and far-off games during all sorts of days and times once reserved for fam-ily affairs. In the end, learning how to kick with the left foot or shoot a jump shot will never build up the average child's sense of self or con-nectedness the way labor-intensive chores once did. The fact that things like canning benefit the group, not just the individual, just fur-ther underscores how shallow an answer American's came up with when they asked themselves, "So what should our girls do with all their free time?"

That is not to say that the great gains in sports for girls should be brushed aside. Anyone who has seen a six-year-old master the art of riding a two-wheel bike knows what a great confidence builder any kind of physical achievement can be. But the excessive attention paid these unnecessary, albeit fun, games for both boys and girls has created a terrible imbalance within the average American family. Parents spend ungodly amounts of time running their children to sporting activities, but even then, they have little or no direct interaction with their child. Weekdays they are off making as much money as possible so their kids can afford good clothes, great schools, and extra training in everything from SATs to lacrosse. Everything centers around the child, but in a way that creates dependence, not independence—a skewed sense of self-worth, not true self-esteem.

In the early 1970s, the Genesko family of Woodbridge, New Jersey, decided to make the swimming career of their eldest daughter, Lynn, the top priority in their life. She won national races, became a confident leader, and secured one of the first college scholarships ever granted a girl. But when she burned out on the laps and competition at age eighteen, she dropped out of college, lost her scholarship, and went home to a family adrift after years of sacrificing nearly everything for the Olympic dream of one child. One of Lynn's sisters (the middle daughter), who hated the meets and endless drives to practices, no longer speaks to most of the family. Lynn now realizes that they all made a mistake when they placed her at the center of things for so long.[14]

Being indulged is a far cry from being essential, and yet that is the switch American families have pulled on their children—to their great detriment. At first glance all this attention may seem ideal for building strong spirits, but somehow girls, in particular, continue to struggle with body image and general self-esteem issues on an astounding scale. Connie Sullivan's family never made it to her badminton games, but as a girl she never felt unloved, and always felt needed. Their demand that she carry her own weight (plus some) motivated her to take on a paper route at a time when girls rarely did such things. She participated in all sorts of activities at school—tennis, badminton, theater—but she always had her special interests in perspective. They were things she did for herself, never at the expense of the household unit.

So the question becomes, How can American parents make their girls feel essential again on the home front without bringing back the oppressive patterns of the past? American culture has worked so hard to broaden opportunities outside the home for its daughters, but for the benefits to be fully felt, we must now grapple with girls' loss of place within the home over the last two hundred years.

Since girls and women have been at the heart of the domestic cycle for so long, it is best to begin with them and eventually work outward. If Americans can get at what was wrong with past patterns and what was constructive, they can initiate a new cycle that involves sons and

daughters. First, parents must bust through stereotypes and fears re-
garding girls and domestic work. Ideally, a gender-neutral answer will
emerge that centers on *children* participating rather than on sex-based
role-playing.

Most children's lives today lack balance precisely because so much
centers on what they need. They float like satellites outside the one
world they most long to be a part of: home. How can parents bring
them back in without cutting them off from the great opportunities
that lie outside the door? On one level it was shameful that Connie and
her sister had to stay home from school to iron. Why not her brothers?
Why any of them? But on another level it placed the needs of the
household above the needs of the individual, a concept many American
families have lost touch with.

Most of the journals and letters of girls like Mollie, who lived outside
their parents' world, have a drifty, disconnected quality to them. They
chat of dolls when a war is blazing around them. They write of their
parents, but in a remote way. But in the writings of the girls who
played vital roles in their household economies, the prose jumps. They
may complain of exhaustion, but it is often a tiredness laced with
pride. Again and again they give detailed accounts of what their parents did every day. They noticed how hard their mother and father
worked, and constantly commented on how much they loved them. It
is this love and respect that fueled their desire to do their part, and unlike many girls today, they had a clear picture of precisely what that
part was.

That is not to say any child should return to factories or hours of
fieldwork. In many instances a daughter's assigned "part" was narrow
in the most damaging sense of the word. But a look into the world of
an eighteenth-century girl, a slave child, or a daughter of the Depression shows there are many ways to balance the private and public responsibilities of a child.

This book examines the lives of fifteen girls who lived in America
from colonial times to the present. The portraits close in on their early
years, ages six to fourteen, when their ideas of duty and self remained
in flux. I discovered their voices in the Schlesinger Library of the Radcliffe Institute at Harvard University, the Library of Congress, in small
archival collections, in books, and in personal interviews. The end
product is a nonfiction history, not a novel, thus I could not make up
details that did not exist in the historical record. At points readers may
wish they knew more about a particular character's day-to-day life, but
if it was not in what she left behind, I could not include it.

"My girls" certainly do not represent every type of girlhood, but they reflect a large enough swath that their experiences can be used as a starting point for a discussion on how to bring daughters back into the flow of American home life. Can we find a balance between the drudgery of the past and isolating patterns of the present? Can we make a girl feel essential again without denying her the right to define herself? Lizzie, Lucy, Mary Ellen, Harriet, Louisa, Mollie, Ethel, Amanda, Connie, Tina, Beverly, Lynn, Meggy, Ally, and Sarah may have some answers.

Section One

DUTIFUL DAUGHTERS
1797 TO 1861

Lizzie, Lucy, Mary Ellen, Harriet, Louisa, and Mollie

For most of human history parents have watched many of their children die young. As late as the eighteenth century, one in every three children died in their first year and only about fifty percent of those survivors reached their twenty-first birthday. For a long time historians, such as Philippe Aries in his groundbreaking book *Centuries of Childhood*, believed that such relentless losses made adults skittish about forming emotional attachments too early. Aries argued that mothers and fathers rarely connected to their babies the way adults do today, remaining distant until their child reached the age of three when they had some chance of making it.

More recently, scholars, such as Nicholas Orme in his book *Medieval Children*, have refuted Aries's conclusions, believing that these families were "ourselves five hundred or a thousand years ago."[1] That may have been true on an emotional level, but when it came to the reality of day-to-day living, there was butter to churn, water to haul, firewood to collect, and more. Parents may have accepted childhood as a special stage with special needs, but they also had a practical bent. The sooner a child made himself or herself useful the better.

By the time Europeans began to settle more permanently in America in the 1700s,[2] life for the average daughter in rural areas remained defined by her usefulness to others. By the time she was eight or nine, she often spent her youth chopping, pounding, lifting, and stirring. It could take an afternoon just to churn the butter for the next day. Most farm families had so many chores they had no time to eat when they woke up in the morning. After a cup of beer or cider, they would set to work. Perhaps by mid-morning they would take a break to eat a meal of eggs, corn mush, salt pork, molasses, and cider. Children often sat separately or stood quietly at the main table.[3]

In more urban areas girls were less weighed down by domestic chores. In the case of Lizzie Perkins, the young daughter of a well-to-do Boston merchant, slaves performed the bulk of the cooking and sewing, and the family often bought what it did not make from people such as the milk-and-butter man. Lizzie had enough free time to build a "museum" with her cousin Jim out of all the rare objects her father brought back from his travels or received from traders, such as a cup made from lava or an ear of corn from Cicero's village in Italy. She engaged in such fanciful play until she was about eleven but then quickly switched to more adult duties, including caring for her sick mother and serving as chief hostess at the main table. While she spent hours mastering cross-stitch, her cousin Jim was groomed to work in the family business and was eventually shipped off to the China office.[4]

Jim needed an education. Jim needed to understand trade. Lizzie needed just enough skills to run a household.

As Barbara Solomon points out in her book, *In the Company of Educated Women*, "usefulness was the measure of all learning" for girls in eighteenth-century America.[5] Some of the more fortunate daughters, like Lizzie, attended Dame Schools, where older women took the children into their homes and taught them how to write, and, on occasion, to read. Lizzie proved especially lucky and acquired both basic skills and a deep love for performing dramatic plays in front of her Scottish grandmother. In many religious households daughters were taught to read so they could study the Bible and eventually teach their own children to do the same.

Thomas Jefferson, who was president during Lizzie's childhood, left a detailed record of what he expected of his own daughters. His advice provides a splendid glimpse into the general tone of the times when it came to raising young girls. While serving as ambassador to France, he often wrote to his Polly (later called Mary) back in the states. He urged her not to

suffer yourself to be angry with any body, that you give your playthings to those who want them, that you do whatever any body desires of you that is right, that you never tell stories, never beg for any thing, mind your books and your work when your aunt tells you, never play but when she permits you, nor go where she forbids you; remember, too, as a constant charge, not to go out without your bonnet, because it will make you very ugly, and then we shall not love you so much. If you always practice these lessons we shall continue to love you as we do now and it is impossible to love you more.[6]

Like Jefferson, Lizzie's father, John Perkins Sr., expected his daughter to be a dutiful helper. Her ultimate charge and the ultimate charge of most girls in New England in 1797: "Do what any body desires of you." Personal aspirations and agendas were not encouraged.

This attitude held firm through much of the nineteenth century, with slavery offering the best example of the darkest aspects of the culture of usefulness. Harriet Jacobs and her daughter Louisa, who lived on a plantation in Georgia in the 1830s, were valued solely on the basis of their productivity and often were treated no better than farm animals. When Harriet's dead father lay in wake a mile down the road from the Georgia plantation where she worked, the young slave's obligation to pick flowers for her mistress' table kept her from paying her last respects. After she escaped to Boston, she had to watch as her own daughter spent her youth running errands for white people, who did not care enough to give her decent clothes.[7]

Such horrible extremes make it difficult to embrace any aspect of the domestic culture in America at that time. But girls like Mary Ellen Todd, who went West to Oregon with her family in 1852, offer uplifting examples of how heavy obligations in the right environment can actually boost self-esteem. As she gathered feed and water, cared for her ailing parents, and cooked, Mary Ellen's confidence grew. She never felt like a cog in a production process, rather, beloved and admired for her skills.[8]

Thousands of miles to the east in Alexandria, Virginia, Mollie Gregory had no physical chores because, like Lizzie Perkins, her wealthy father could buy many of the things rural families had to make and divvied up the remaining work among his slaves. On a certain level Mollie represents the most modern daughter in this section because her parents treated her as someone who needed protecting and coddling rather then someone who should contribute in a vital way. Yet like Lizzie and Mary Ellen, Mollie still had to play the role of dutiful daughter. Anything she might want to do—from paint to write—took a backseat to whatever her parents expected of her. Their needs remained more important than her needs.[9]

A glimmer of a more balanced life began to open up in unexpected ways for girls around the middle of the nineteenth century. Lucy Larcom sacrificed much of her youth to the mills of Lowell, Massachusetts so her widowed mother could feed and house their large family. But even as she labored to meet the needs of the household, she managed to make a name for herself in the world of letters. She worked ten-hour days then attended literary meetings in the evenings, where famous poets such as John Greenleaf Whittier took note of her work. Poorly schooled because of her mill life, Lucy began to aspire to a better education, and even had thoughts of a career centered on teaching and writing.

In many of their journals, nineteenth-century daughters chronicle their march away from the duty-bound life into a world where personal achievement outside the home begins to matter. Everything they did, including furthering their education, remained contingent on fulfilling their family obligations first, but at least girls like Lucy, and even Mary Ellen Todd—who learned to crack the whip and set the oxen going—began to peek around the corner. They realized they could be essential at home and still aspire to meet essential needs within themselves.

1797. Most history books mention little about this relatively stable period just after the Revolution and prior to the War of 1812. Boston, once the largest British city in North America, was still a major port by the late eighteenth century, just behind New York and Philadelphia in size and importance. Nearly 25,000 people shared Lizzie's hometown.[1]

The area's deep, well-sheltered harbor made it an ideal hub for all kinds of commerce. During Lizzie's youth, forty wharves took in whalers and clipper ships laden with goods from the Far East. Great salt marshes, now filled, rimmed the waterfront. The downtown area lay tied to the mainland by just a strip of dirt, now part of Washington Street.[2]

While her rural counterparts sustained themselves on basic fare, Lizzie was exposed to all sorts of exotic foods and flavors, such as cinnamon. She probably attended large public gatherings on a regular basis for celebrations, including the launching of the USS Constitution in 1797.[3] (Paul Revere cast the great ship's copper bolts and spikes.)

Very few American girls in eighteenth-century America could read and write, which helps account for the dearth of firsthand accounts from daughters raised on farms. Lizzie Perkins's tale of her youth is simply written by today's standards, but it is a remarkable achievement given the education available to her.[4] While researching at the Schlesinger Library in Cambridge, Massachusetts, I did come across other accounts written by girls who grew up in eighteenth-century America, including the well-known Anna Green Winslow, but Lizzie's more detailed record of her household duties and her portrait of slaves at work in the kitchen set her story apart.

A sweet, somewhat pampered Boston girl, Lizzie is hardly representative of the daughters of her time. But the fact she remained such a duty-bound girl in one of the freest, wealthiest, most educated of environments says volumes about domestic obligations in general in America in 1797.

1797

LIZZIE
Do What Anybody Desires of You

John Perkins Sr., a trader in Boston in 1797, had a mild wife named Sarah, who hardly relished all of the characters from overseas who often paraded through their living room on Pearl Street. But he could see that his eight-year-old daughter, Lizzie, gravitated toward the exotic and listened with rapt attention as men told of beheadings in France or Grandmother Perkins went on about sending her great easy chair "to help in the bringing back [of] the wounded from Bunker Hill. . . . It was returned to me drenched in blood," the old woman said with grim detail.[5]

As a child, Lizzie only half understood what they were talking about—wars, revolutions, men lost at sea—but the stories about adventure and duty often ran through her mind whenever the adults shooed her into the kitchen, where she spent most of her time playing and eating when she was not at the Dame School. No one under the age of eleven was allowed at the main dinner table (6).

One night in particular, she recalled later in her journal, she cried when sent to bed as visitors related their adventures. Agents from the Northwest Company named McGilvrary and McTavish had stopped in. "My father used to carry their furs from the Northwest Coast of China. McGilvrary gave my mother the skin of a grizzly bear he killed with a knife. They were going from one post to another when it attacked them" (22).

While Lizzie did not get the bear skin, she did accumulate all sorts of strange trinkets and collectibles, which she and a cousin, Jim, made into a small museum in her house. They showcased bear teeth, Italian sonnets, and lava cups along the tiny shelves. In a careful hand, they wrote small cards for each item. Against the backdrop of the Perkins's house, with its oak panels and marble mantelpiece from England, the children's small museum probably seemed quaint to passing adults, but to Lizzie it was one way to reach out into the exotic maritime culture that surrounded her (18).

She knew from a very early age that she would never directly participate in that culture. Lizzie's cousins, Jim and John, eventually sailed to China to work in the Perkins's office there, but she stayed tight within her domestic realm.

Unlike most of the farm girls of her generation, Lizzie's feminine duties did not involve much hard labor. From age six or so she spent several hours every day working on a sampler—a piece of needlework that required expertise in lettering, stitching, and patience. Daughters from wealthier families were expected to master a wider range of stitches and produce more refined samplers. As one ditty of the time exclaims:

> A Sampler resembles an elegant mind,
> Whose passions by reason subdu'd and refin'd,
> Move only in lines of affection and duty,
> Reflecting a picture of order and beauty.[6]

While Lizzie's less well-to-do counterparts kneaded, churned and stirred, she cross-stitched, backstitched, chain stitched, and fishbone stitched, and, if she had an experienced teacher, maybe even tried out Algerian eye. To complete a decent sampler, Lizzie had to read and write at a modest level. Her proud parents may have framed her work and hung it in the parlor for visitors to see. They were not showcasing her literacy, however, as much as her skill with a needle. The conventional wisdom of the time: The more sophisticated her sampler the better prepared she would be to run an organized, tidy household and mark her future family's linens.

Despite the many months, even years, that Lizzie must have spent from the age of six to ten working on her samplers, she makes no mention of them in her journal. She wrote just one paragraph on Mrs. Cranch's Dame School, where she probably did most of her needlework. The highlight of her time there: "The pretty view from the River looking down from the bridge."[7] Perhaps the daily lessons in proper needlework and letters seemed too ordinary to mention, but there is no doubt any eight-year-old girl would bristle under a teacher's constant demand to stitch meticulously for hours. Silence may have been the strongest statement she allowed herself to make about this key aspect of her day-to-day life.

During her free time she played at rag dolls with her younger sisters under the eye of the slave Mummy Tucker. The older woman would work to keep the fire going while cooking up squash, soup, bread, and meat for the household. "There was a large fireplace with a crane and a kettle always hanging," Lizzie recalled. "She cooked beafsteak or mutton chop in the grying pan. We had milk and biscuits. We had clams given to us in the spring to 'purify the blood'" (20).

Some mornings Lizzie and her sisters would walk along the wharves at the end of their block. The salt marsh breezes off Boston Harbor helped clear their heads of the stench that often built up along the crowded, feces-strewn streets. With her long hair pulled above her head and her petite frame in an adult-style woolen dress and bonnet, Lizzie must have cut a fragile figure as she moved among the brusque sailors and silent slaves who worked the docks. The ships pulling in usually carried finished goods, such as porcelain or textiles. American ships pulling out generally had raw material on board, such as molasses and timber.[8]

Lizzie seemed to care little for such details. She barely mentions the ships that dominated her landscape and her father's business. Instead, she dwelled on the poetry and plays she loved. In addition to the Dame School, John Perkins sent his daughter to a special tutor named Mrs. Paine, "a Jewess, a handsome woman, a good woman, a woman of taste," Lizzie said. Unlike Mrs. Cranch, the tutor read English poetry "and encouraged us to read it. She allowed us to pick out pieces to learn. Cowper was a favorite, and we used to read Goldsmith and Burns." She expecially loved to read Robert Burns to the all-girl class.[9]

Mrs. Paine may have also used the *New England Primer*, first printed in 1690 but still widely used throughout the Northeast a hundred years later. Girls like Lizzie would practice their penmanship and spelling by copying out sayings such as "Train up a child in the way he should go, and when he is old he will not depart from it."[10]

Lizzie's family also encouraged her to engage with the English language on a more sophisticated level than just learning to write her name or spell out a poem on her sampler. Her maternal grandmother Elliot, who hailed from Scotland and sang forth Burns's poetry with an authentic burr, often invited Lizzie and her sisters over to her large garden to stage plays. With a purring tone, she would walk them through their parts for plays such as *Search after Happiness*, by the well-known New England playwright Miss Hannah More.[11]

"Eliza Otis [a friend] and I were shepherdesses, in white dresses trimmed with flowers and crooks in our hands." Each in turn related her search for happiness in various directions:

> Lizzie: "Learning is all the fair Cleora's aim;
> She seeks the loftest pinnacle of Fame:
> Would she the privilege of Man invade?
> Science for female minds was never made.
> Taste, Elegance, and Talents may be ours,
> But Learning suits not our less vigorous powers:
> Learning but roughens, polished taste refines . . ."[12]

As such excerpts show, even as Lizzie broadened her mind in ways few of her contemporaries could ever hope to, she was reminded that such gains were forms of refinement only. Lizzie could never expect to follow in the footsteps of her male cousins who headed for college while she took on an ever-increasing number of domestic duties at home.

By the time she was twelve, Lizzie had no time for museums, long walks, plays or samplers. She had moved to the main table:

If my mother was sick, I used to take the whole care of her. I had a truckle bed in the room and was up and down in the night, making poultices and doing all the work of a sick nurse, and nobody thought it anything out of the way. I helped to take care of the younger children, and when the seamstress came to make our clothes, I worked as hard as she did, and harder too. I kept at it as long as I could see to thread a needle. When I was 12-years-old, father made me take the head of the table one day when he had a dinner party and mother could not come down. (24)

Though a slight girl herself, Lizzie had the social energy her mother lacked. "She never wanted to stir if she could help it," the daughter recalled (24), and then lapses into mostly silence about this primary figure in her life. In general it was her father who looked after her education, her appearance (he even bought combs for her hair so she would be as stylish as some of the neighborhood girls), and her duties in the household. As a prosperous merchant and trader, John Perkins must have rejoiced at his maturing daughter's growing role. Finally, he had the female figure he needed to cater to his many guests and to accompany him on his trips throughout New England, where he had part ownership in an iron ore mine on Lake Champlain (24). Now Lizzie received all the exotic presents of furs and coral, but she no longer had the time to turn them into playthings.

As an adult woman looking back on her life, Lizzie did not view her upbringing as oppressive or confining. She did applaud the fact that children of both sexes mingled more easily in the early nineteenth century than they did during her girlhood, but in the end, even though America's daughters seemed to "learn a great deal" in this freer environment, they were "not thought to have any duties except to have a good time and everybody plans for that; and so when they are married, they break down" (30).

Lizzie had learned by the age of twelve that "her principle was duty not pleasure. [She] was to ask what was right, not what was pleasant" (30). She took great pride in the fact that her father wanted her company on his long trips and that her mother welcomed her help as seamstress, nurse, and hostess. From the vantage point of the twenty-first century, it is hard not to see that her caretaker role cut her off from the education and careers enjoyed by her male relatives. It is easy to assume she felt deprived. But Lizzie herself expressed no such longings and seemed to blossom under the basic knowledge that her parents valued her contributions.

1830–1840. The Industrial Revolution took firm root in the United States during a very volatile period. From 1830–1840 Native Americans died by the thousands as U.S. soldiers tried to herd them onto reservations. Northerners and Southerners continued to debate the issue of slavery with a viciousness that would eventually result in the Civil War. Against this backdrop, businessmen began transforming the face of American industry, especially on the East Coast, with mechanized factories.

Little Lucy Larcom found herself caught in this web of change when her father died suddenly in 1830 and left the family with no means of support. By the time the Larcom girls moved to Lowell, Massachusetts, in 1833 to work in the factories, the owners had built twenty-two mills in the cow fields and hired thousands of employees.[1] Of course the Boston businessmen had not expected to use young children. Unlike their British counterparts, where the Industrial Revolution had first taken hold much earlier in cities such as Manchester, the Americans believed they could build a decent town and a decent work environment along with a profitable factory. Their mill hands would not live in the squalor that plagued the British industrial towns. With the help of boardinghouse mothers, such as Mrs. Larcom, and strict regulations about age, dress, behavior, and education, these Boston patriarchs believed they could build efficient, prosperous mills and an upstanding, well-dressed workforce.

In the beginning, most of the girls were fourteen or older and only stayed for two to three years.[2] They made money so a brother could go to school or they could have a decent dowry. Most had something to go home to if the millwork became too much for them. But as the 1830s gave way to the 1840s, the Boston owners became more profit oriented and less paternalistic about protecting their girls. Eleven-year-olds, like Lucy, began to show up on the work floor for ten-hour days. Hours lengthened for everyone, and wages dropped. By the time Lucy was in her teens, some of the girls had begun to organize and strike. Sometimes work stopped for days, costing the owners thousands of dollars, but in the end the young women had to return to their jobs. Immigrants desperate for any kind of work started competing for their slots. By the 1850s, the experiment at Lowell had succumbed to the same problems that had befallen industry in Great Britain: Overworked, underpaid, unskilled laborers became stuck in a grueling desperate cycle.

Lucy escaped these nasty shifts by heading West to be a teacher. She had already established herself as a reputable writer and eventually published a popular autobiography, A New England Girlhood. On so many levels her life represented all that was awful and yet freeing about American life for daughters in the mid-nineteenth century.

LUCY
Dutiful Helper

The family vegetable garden needed weeding so Captain Benjamin Lar-com marched a handful of his ten children up the hill. He doled out pennies for each finished section and served up a mixture of molasses and water to help offset the heat of the New England summer. His sec-ond youngest daughter, Lucy, age six, spent more time climbing apple trees and staring out to sea than clearing rows. Her sisters jingled their coins at her when they were done, but she did not mind. No amount of money could replace the joy she felt while roaming the beaches and fields near her Beverly, Massachusetts, home in 1830. "I greatly en-joyed the freedom of the solitary explorer among the seashells and wildflowers," she recalled. "There were wonders everywhere. I picked up a starfish on the beach (we called them five fingers). I overtook horseshoe crabs. These were also pretty canary-colored cockle shells and tiny purple mussels. There was no end to the interesting things I found when I was trusted to go down to the edge of the tide alone."[3]

For the first ten years of her life, Lucy's "tether was a long one" (88). She had her share of chores—watching baby Octavia, fetching milk from the farmhouse every morning, shoveling hot coals from the oven—but they were jobs that made her feel part of the flow. "We smaller girls thought it a great privilege to be allowed to watch the oven till the roof of it was 'white-hot' so that the coals could be shov-eled out" (52). "Everybody about us worked, and we expected to take hold of our part while young. I think we were rather eager to begin, for we believed that work would make men and women of us" (120).

But from an early age Lucy bristled at doing many of the traditional female chores, like sewing or knitting, that her older sisters excelled at. Again and again, Lida and Emeline tried to show their younger sibling the finer points of working lace or sewing clothes, but Lucy balked. Her neck muscles would tighten; her foot would begin to dance. Her eyes longed for the details of the landscape not the nuances of cloth or yarn. As the second youngest of seven girls, Lucy benefited from the fact that her sisters were extremely skilled tailors. The family was well-off enough that the labor of a six-year-old did not tip the balance one way or the other. With her attractive sisters clucking their tongues in disapproval, the plain-looking, awkward Lucy usually managed to escape to her beloved fields and beaches.

The family found ways to turn her energetic disposition and physical strength to the groups' advantage, usually by assigning her outdoor manual tasks such as carrying the heavy milk pails or chasing after the family baby. Her brother Jonathan often had her walk the four miles to the old farmstead with him to see their father's relatives and visit with the cousins. They would spend the night and join in feeding the pigs and chickens as though it were all part of being on a holiday. Back home, Lucy did manage to settle down enough to thread needles for her half blind aunt Stanley, but that was only because she loved to hear the old woman's stories of the early generations of Larcoms who had come with the Puritan settlement at the Massachusetts Bay Colony in 1630.[4] Indeed, Lucy could sit for hours if there was a story about—either in her own head, in a book, or in a conversation going on around her.

By the time she was seven she gave in to some of her sister's demands and learned to knit because she realized she could read a book as she clicked her needles. Social conventions demanded that she should knit enough stockings to fill a pillowcase before she married, but her sack stayed half empty. As the plainest looking of the seven daughters and the least skilled with a needle, Lucy knew her prospects for marriage were slim and, by age eight or so, had already concluded she was destined to live the life of an old maid.

And yet Lucy's mind reached where her sisters' could not. She learned to read before she was five and had a tremendous memory, particularly for hymns, which she sang to herself all day. But while sewing and knitting were considered essential skills for all the Larcom girls, an education beyond the basics of penmanship and reading the Bible was not. They did attend a school of sorts, run by their aunt Hannah, above Captain Larcom's general store in the heart of Beverly. The kids would scamper up a ladder, then spend the day watching the older woman cook or spin on her flax wheel. Somewhere in between her chores she taught them their letters and how to read and kept the toddlers out of trouble. The classroom text: the Bible.

Lucy's large family and their solid financial situation made it possible for her to sneak off and write poetry or plays, but her parents and teacher made it clear that her writing talent was not a useful skill, like cooking or knitting was, and should be explored only as a form of leisure. "My mother, fortunately, was sensible enough never to flatter me or let me be flattered about my scribbling. It never was allowed to hinder any work I had to do."[5]

When words failed her, Lucy often turned to watercolors. Her sister Emeline, who was also an avid reader, excellent writer, and fine sketch artist, gave her paint and paper and encouraged her artistic yearnings. Sometimes they would work together to capture the light on the inlet that flowed by their town, but most often Lucy worked her brushes alone. As one of the older girls, Emeline felt duty bound to help around the house as much as possible. Poems and paintings were for the young.

In the end, the hill overlooking the sea from Beverly proved a rich classroom and playground for Lucy Larcom and her siblings. The gray seaside lichens and carpet of bluegill entertained them in ways children today would find hard to understand. Lucy and her friends and family believed that God revealed himself through nature and to study His handiwork was to know the world. Simply peering over the stonewall that paralleled the shore allowed Lucy to "feel the freedom of the hill. . . . If I had opened my eyes upon this planet elsewhere than in this northeastern corner of Massachusetts, elsewhere than on this green rocky strip of shore between Beverly Bridge and Misery Islands, it seems to me as if I must have been somebody else and not myself. These gray ledges hold me by the roots as they do the bayberry bushes, the sweet-fern and the rock saxifrage" (17).

But Lucy was not destined to stay in Beverly. The loosely structured, safe world her parents had built for her and her nine siblings broke when Captain Larcom died in 1831. Lucy was seven years old.

Her father had made his career as a sea captain but quit when war broke out between England and the United States in 1812. With the British searching and seizing American vessels, the hazardous profession of seaman became that much riskier and Larcom wanted out. He had saved enough money to buy some land and a home in Beverly a few miles from the homestead where he had grown up. He used his connections and cash to open a general store that carried many of the exotic items he once sailed around the world on his ships, including silk, coffee, and chocolates. A handsome but stern and aloof man, the captain's word was law in the Larcom household. His wife, Lois Barrett Larcom, had a soft, friendly way about her that helped take the edge off the father's military demeanor, but, as things soon proved, Lois was ill suited to take charge of things.

She relished her role as well-to-do housekeeper and mother of a large family, but like most women of her generation, she had no career outside the household and never expected to be the primary provider for her children. Fortunately for the Larcom girls, their father had encouraged self-sufficiency in all of his offspring and had most of his daughters learn the finer points of tailoring. When he died, the older girls—Lida, Abigail, and Emeline—started doing work for hire for area families. Lucy, now nearly eight, was expected to take on more of their domestic chores.

Lucy was too young to know fully all that had been lost with her father's passing. As her brother held her up so she could peer into the casket, she remained convinced her father was in a deep sleep. His face had the same pale, stern countenance it had carried at their long Sunday meetings. The family would stand in their Sabbath-best clothes and listen obediently as the captain went on at length about the scriptures and whatever the minister might have discussed that day at the general meeting. Fidgety Lucy managed to endure these long diatribes by humming hymns in her head. She had memorized more than one hundred of them and could run through them for hours. No matter how jumpy she might feel, she knew enough to say nothing. "My most vivid recollection of his living face is as I saw it reflected in a mirror while he stood thus praying. His closed eyes, the paleness and seriousness of his countenance awed me" (24).

Now the man who ran the Sunday meetings, provided all of their income, and set all of the rules was gone. Since the family owned their house and some land and the girls had some marketable skills, the family had a chance of managing in Beverly, but somehow Lois Larcom could not sustain a budget. The eldest boy, eighteen-year-old Benjamin, followed in his father's footsteps and went to sea on a merchant vessel. "My mother looked upon him as her future stay and support" (143).

But pirates attacked Benjamin's ship and set it afire. "The crew was fastened down in the hold. One small skylight had accidentally been overlooked by the freebooters. The captain discovered it and making his way through it to the deck, succeeded in putting out the fire, else vessel and sailors would have sunk together" (144). Benjamin returned to Beverly happy to be alive and certain he wanted nothing more to do with the sea. He apprenticed to a carpenter, which took care of his own basic needs but provided nothing for the extended family.

I was beginning to be made aware that poverty was a possible visitation to our own household; and that in our Cape Ann corner of Massachusetts, we might find it neither comfortable nor picturesque. After my father's death, our way of living never luxurious, grew more and more frugal. Now and then I heard mysterious allusions to "the wolf at the door"; and it was whispered to escape that, to escape him, we might all have to turn our backs upon the home where we were born, and find our safety in the busy world, working among strangers for our daily bread. Before I had reached my tenth year, I began to have rather disturbed dreams of what it might soon mean for me to "earn my own living." (136)

Lois Larcom simply lacked the skills to take charge of the household finances. With food from their garden and income from her daughters' needlework, they could have managed. But Mrs. Larcom continued to set a relatively fancy table and to expect a certain quality of clothing for her children. She purchased books for the family library, an extravagance even in the best of times.

The family hung on for three years, but the combination of Lois Larcom's incompetence and her husband's debt of $500, a considerable sum for the early nineteenth century, forced the captain's wife to sell the family home and land.[6] They had to move on—but to what? At one point Lucy's father had thought of shifting the family to Lowell because he knew his five youngest daughters could work in the new textile mills in the event he could not provide for them all. With no clear ideas of her own, Lois Larcom turned to her husband's former backup plan and decided to move most of her family to Lowell. Some of the older children stayed behind either because they could support themselves or because they had married, but Lucy and four of her sisters made the big journey from rural Beverly to Lowell's industrial world of steam-powered machines, bosses, and time clocks.

Mrs. Larcom signed on as a boardinghouse supervisor. One thing she knew how to do was run a large household. In exchange for overseeing a group of New England farm girls who had traded the unforgiving fields of Maine and Vermont for the steady wages of the mills, Lois would receive housing and a small stipend. If several of her older girls went to work as well, she could afford to have her three younger ones— Lida, Lucy, and Octavia—stay in school.

Lucy was ten years old when she said good-bye to the sea from a hill in Beverly. She was old enough to know she would miss her garret and her long walks to the Larcom farmstead, but she was still young enough to be thrilled, in a frightening sort of way, by the big changes ahead. She knew she was trading a quiet life by the beaches for the bustle of a mill town along the banks of the Merrimack River. Somehow she must have also sensed that her responsibilities would change with the territory. If she was not being sent off to get the milk from the barnyard, then exactly what was she going to be doing in this new world?

At first she and her sister Lida sewed and sewed and sewed. All of the beds at the boardinghouse required sheets, which required seams. "It was warm weather, and that made it the more tedious, for we wanted to be running about the fields. One day, in sheer desperation, we dragged a sheet up with us into an apple tree . . . and sat and sewed there through the summer afternoon, beguiling the irksomeness of our task by telling stories and guessing riddles."[7]

By fall they had moved into their new brick home, "which was quickly filled with a large feminine family" (152). All the new clapboard stores and houses gave the town a slapdash look so it lacked the ambiance of historic Beverly, but Lowell did have a hum about it that Lucy found exciting. Not that she had much time for exploring. When she was not at school, she was doing chores for her mother back at the boardinghouse, including making beds, trimming lamps, and washing lots and lots of dishes. "As a child the gulf between little girlhood and young womanhood had always looked to me very wide. I supposed we should get across it by some sudden jump by and by. But among these new companions of all ages, from 15 to 30 years, we slipped into womanhood without knowing when or how" (152).

While she took on a woman's burden at home, she struggled with a grade school curriculm at school. "For the first time in our lives my little sister and I became pupils in a grammar school for both girls and boys, taught by a man!" (150). Her teacher was a fierce figure who had no patience for Lucy's poor understanding of mathematics, which Aunt Hannah had never gotten around to in her makeshift kitchen classes. All the strange mathematical symbols confused Lucy. She could form her letters nicely but had no idea what to do with the straight line with one dot above it and one below. The man's deep voice startled her. When he announced that she would have to move back a few grades, she could barely handle the shame of sitting among much younger schoolmates.

Back home, Lucy escaped the strain of school, chores, and the hordes of girls that swarmed through their house every evening by skipping down to the river. She marveled at the different texture of the water, the unusual flowers, the animal life. This was not the sea, but

something rare in its own right. "To live beside a river had been to me a
child's dream of romance. Rivers, as I pictured them, came down from
the mountains, and were born in the clouds" (162). She scampered
around the rocks at Pawtucket Falls, where the roar from the water
had a different note than the waves of the sea. She spotted harebell
blossoms for the first time and fish in the pools. No matter how hard
the day, Lucy could always feel free along the Merrimack.

Despite the new house and income, the Larcoms still struggled. Lucy,
as the second to youngest child, felt she burdened her family. Her
mother never complained and even bragged to a neighbor that "I could
not spare a single one of my children" (162), but she felt the pinch. No
matter how hard she tried to economize, it just did not come naturally
to her, and she continued to spend too much on fine food for the table
and decorations and extra odds and ends for the house. Lois had managed to keep three of her girls out of the mills, while Emeline and Abigail worked, but their combined incomes were still not enough.
Someone else had to enter the mill.

Lida was older, but Lucy was stronger. Large for her age and sturdy,
Lucy was picked to go to work. The mill supervisor balked at taking in
an eleven-year-old and reminded the mother that by law her daughter
had to attend school for at least three months. So Lucy went to work
under a nine-month contract to replace bobbins from 5 A.M. to 7 P.M.
Monday through Friday for about $1.50 a week.[8]

She began her new life with a "light heart." The thrill of escaping the
awkward classroom situation and

the novelty of it made it seem easy, and it really was not hard, just to change
the bobbins on the spinning frames every three quarters of an hour or so, with
half a dozen other little girls who were doing the same thing. And for a little
while it was only a new amusement. . . . There was a great deal of play mixed
in with it. The intervals were spent frolicking around among the spinning-
frames, teasing and talking to the older girls or entertaining ourselves with
games and stories in the corner.[9]

She even managed to find time to roam the banks of the Merrimack,
only now she did it at 4 A.M. instead of 4 P.M. "We were children still,
whether at school or at work, and Nature still held us close to her
motherly heart" (163).

But eventually the buzzing, hissing, whizzing of the pulleys and
rollers and spindles and flyers knocked all the fun out of everything.
For a girl raised on sea sounds and wildflowers, the machinery seemed
like some horrible, blasting beast. Sometimes during a lull, she would

go with a young friend and peer through the blinds on the door over-looking the enormous waterwheel. The river pressed against the great circle and set the whole thing in motion. "It was so huge that we could only watch a few of its spokes at a time, and part of its dripping rim, moving with a slow, measured strength through the darkness that shut it in. . . . The mill itself had its lessons for us. But it was not, and could not be, the right sort of life for a child" (154–155). But Lois Larcom needed that $1.50.

When the summer flowers next blossomed along the Merrimack, Lucy's family took her out of the mill so she could attend school for three months. She jumped at the chance to leave her job as a doffer of bobbins for the once-hated benches of school. She applied herself with renewed vigor and began to decipher the plus and minus signs, the quirky division symbol, and the tricks of math in general. Her reading and writing, always strong, advanced well past her grade level. She not only joined her age group, she surpassed them, and had come to thirst after any kind of learning she could acquire. In less than twenty months, Lucy had made up years of lost ground. The classroom's stern taskmaster declared her ready for high school; an astounding develop-ment for a girl with Lucy's educational background. But her family could not afford to lose her wages for the entire year, so when August gave way to September, Lucy returned to the mill.

This time she regretted leaving her studies and struggled mightily with the tedious work. "The transition from childhood to girlhood, when a little girl has had an almost unlimited freedom of out-of-door life, is practically the toning down of a mild sort of barbarianism" (166). The noise, the sedentary nature of the work, the repetition—it all hammered away at her spirit, but she kept on. Now almost thirteen, she was mature enough to tackle the better paying job of sewer. She donned a work apron like the older girls she used to watch and headed to the sewing rooms where she stitched and ran machines for ten to twelve hours a day. Gone were the days when the family could indulge her need to break from such tedious work. She had to sit and sit and sit. She let her mind roam because her body could not. They were not allowed to bring books in with them, so she would tear out pages of po-etry and paste them on the wall or hide them in a pocket. "I discovered, too, that I could so accustom myself to the noise that it became like a silence to me" (183).

Wrapped in her wall of noise and repetitive motion, Lucy thought she could tune out her feelings of entrapment and accept her lot. On the surface, she succeeded. For the next two years she worked in the mills, arriving on time, working all day, giving her mother her earnings. But she became plagued by headaches and exhaustion. Worried, her family sent her back to Beverly to live with a sister who needed some child care help. For a time the soothing quiet of her hometown brought Lucy back to life, but after just six months or so she became restless. The writer in her missed the stimulation of the larger city: the guest speakers, the public library. Beverly no longer offered a wide enough vista for her literary talent. She decided she "must be where my life could expand" (193). So once again she left the ocean scenes of the seaside town for the clamoring of the textile mills, but this time it was of her own voliation. She wanted to return to make a wage and find a way to educate herself so she could become a self-supporting teacher and writer. Lucy, a sixteen-year-old girl from a puritanical New England village, had something her female ancestors never aspired to: a career plan.

In the older times it was seldom said to little girls, as it always has been said to boys, that they ought to have some definite plan, while they were children, what to be and do when they are grown up. There was usually but one path open before them, to become good wives and housekeepers. And the ambition of most girls was to follow their mother's footsteps in this direction; a natural and laudable ambition. But girls, as well as boys, must often have been conscious of their own peculiar capabilities—must have desired to cultivate and make use of their individual powers. (157)

She joined her sister Emeline as a dresser, one of the highest paying jobs at the mill, but she soon found that once again the noise, lint, and repetition chewed on her nerves. She demoted herself to the cloth room, where a few men and girls measured and baled the finished cloth and entered the final tally into account books.[10] They worked just an eight-hour day and had long spaces of time between the busy spells. Lucy knew it meant less money, but the loss was hers alone since she no longer had to funnel her earnings into the larger Larcom pot. Her mother had given up her life as boardinghouse supervisor in Lowell and returned to Beverly, where she lived with one of her children. Now Lucy paid her own keep and shared a place with her sister.

More than ever before she spent her hours at the mill conjuring up poems in her head or going over something she had read the night before. While she was in Beverly, her sister Emeline and a handful of other mill girls had launched a literary publication, "The Lowell Offering," and had begun a series of weekly meetings. Now at the close of day, Lucy often joined up with other exhausted mill girls to discuss literature they had read or to exchange poems and short items they had written themselves. Some evenings they had guest speakers, such as men involved in the labor movement or the poet John Greenleaf Whittier, who applauded the girls' independence and encouraged their literary efforts.

During one of "The Lowell Offering" get-togethers, Whittier approached Lucy and told her she had a special talent and that she should try to sell some of her writings to journals and newspapers. Lucy the second youngest of ten, the mill girl, the daughter of the fierce captain was too awed to respond. But the famous poet's positive words stayed with her, and she began to conjure up plans that would get her out of Lowell and into a career as a teacher and writer.

Because several of her sisters had married, including Emeline, Lucy was left feeling even more desperate than ever to find her own way. Emeline and her husband George Spaulding encouraged Lucy to go West with them. The new states needed young, strong, educated women like Lucy. She could teach. After ten years among machines and a relentless work schedule, the openness of the prairies seemed enticing, even if it did mean cutting herself off from the literary life she had begun to develop for herself. In 1846 the group began the long journey West by canal boat, train, and carriage.

A girl "often lets her life get broken into fragments among the flimsy trellises of fashion and conventionality, when it might be a perfect thing in the upright beauty of its own consecrated freedom. Yet girlhood seldom appreciates itself. We often hear a girl wishing that she were a boy. That seems so strange. God made no mistake in her creation. He sent her into the world full of power and will to be a helper."[11] Now twenty-one and no longer a girl, Lucy Larcom went West to begin a new phase of her life. She continued to play the role of dutiful helper, only now for her sister's family, but she also began to branch out. With each passing year she became more aware of the duty she bore herself as an independent woman and as a gifted writer.

Lucy learned from her years in the mills that simply meeting the essential needs of one's family could leave a girl spent. To strike a better balance, she took her "peculiar capabilities" more seriously—a remarkable step for a girl of her generation. She marked the beginning of a vanguard of young women, who tried to sustain their roles as dutiful daughters at home even as they reached outward into society "to cultivate their individual powers."

1852. A quarter of a million people made their way to the Pacific coast between 1840 and 1860, most of them men. Initially, a lot of families went because of the promise of farmland, but then news of gold in California reached young men in the East, and from 1849 to 1852, 150,000 of them made the trek. According to Elliott West, the records at Fort Laramie show that 99 children, 119 women and 17,443 men came through in 1850. All told less than 20 percent of the population in the far West was under age fifteen.[1]

Not only were there few children around, those that did live there were expected to labor hard. "Among the young," West writes, "the demands of the frontier ate away at distinctions of age and gender." He adds, "Most families could not afford idle children" (74–75).

Mary Ellen Todd fits into this portrait as a hardworking young girl who did everything she could to help her struggling parents, including chores normally assigned to boys. Later, after she had married and settled down with her own family, Mary Ellen told her pioneer stories to her children and grandchildren. One daughter, Adrietta Applegate Hixon, decided to write down Mary Ellen's amazing narrative, which she completed in 1935 when she was eighty. A small press published On to Oregon *in 1973. Fortunately, Adrietta tried to re-create the various stories precisely as Mary Ellen told them. A wonderful lilt that I find so uplifting and impressive fills the pages of* On to Oregon, *a lasting imprint of one pioneering girl's great contributions and spirit.*

MARY ELLEN
The Power to Set Things Going

The tar smelled and stuck to everything, including her clothes, but nine-year-old Mary Ellen Todd did not mind greasing the wheels, because she could hear their song so clearly: "Going-to-Oregon, Going-to-Oregon, Going-to-Oregon."[2] This messy chore marked the end of the family's months of preparation for their journey West from Arkansas. Her parents kept her busy with small but vital chores, like taking a saw or hammer to her father or looking after baby Cynthia. "Mary Ellen," her mother cried, "won't you finish this churning while I get my soap to boiling; we'll need a lot of soap, you know; also I must finish spinning all those rolls that we have been carding, as we just must take with us plenty of yarn" (17). "Yes, to be sure, I had to wash most of the dishes," Mary Ellen recalled, "but Louvina, who was not past six years of age, sometimes helped me" (17).

She never openly questioned her father's decision to leave their family and friends in 1852, because he had the vague notion that something better might be ahead. Just a few years back Abbott Todd had moved his family from Illinois to Arkansas, though they trekked just a few hundred miles and they had joined his mother, not left her. Now Mary Ellen's stepmother, Angelina Tate, her two younger sisters, and adopted older brother, John, faced more than two thousand miles of walking, much of it over sparsely or unsettled territory.

As the time grew nearer [to leave], excitement increased; I fairly seemed to fly from place to place. Many relatives and friends were deeply interested in the great event, and I sometimes saw them wiping away tears; I did feel some deep regrets about leaving them, but I could not have been hired to stay behind, even though we had heard of the harrowing fates and hair breadth escapes of those who had gone before.

The oxen were all yoked up, one horse saddled, and the last things put into the wagon; still we lingered.

The group of dear ones were standing about, some were crying, and one said, "I know you will all be killed and we shall never see you again." They went from one of us to another sobbing words of endearment and advice. Grandma could only say, "Oh, honey, honey." (20–21)

Mary Ellen wept for a time but by the second or third night of camp the tingle of excitement overcame the tears. She spent hours contemplating the changing landscape and the idea of Oregon, while munching quietly on the last fresh loaf of her grandmother's salt rising bread.

Everything about the journey to Happy Valley, Oregon, was intimidating: the size of the wagon, the extent of the preparation, the intensity of the heat and bugs, and the unpredictability of the Native Americans. In those gentle first weeks, the Todd family traveled alone through settled territory and spring light. But as they closed in on Missouri and the great expanse that lay beyond, they decided to join a wagon train just outside of Independence. Of the one hundred wagons they left with, ninety-six decided the cold Kaw River in eastern Kansas was just one obstacle too many and turned back. That left just four families to handle the awesome task of dismantling and unpacking the wagons so the wagon beds could be used as boats.

The wagon beds had to be taken off, emptied, and turned upside down, caulked and pitched with rosin and tar inside and out, that they might be used as boats. All this caused quite a bit of confusion in camp, as everything had to be taken out and stowed around.

Our wagon beds were drawn up to the water's edge, pushed off into the water, then made secure and loaded up, ready to cross. The wagon gears had to be taken apart and also ferried over.

We first waited on the banks to see them swim the stock across. Father let a man ride one of our horses and he rode the other. All our animals had been gathered up and were browsing about on the banks. The men began rounding them up and closing in on them. The cracking of their whips and lusty, "Ho-ay!, Ho-ay!, Ho-ay!" set them all in motion. Then they were pressed right down to the edge of the water. . . . As they began to strike swimming water, some would turn about and try to come back, but the horseriders with those awful weapons of persuasion prevailed upon the poor beasts to go on. The cattle then soon settled down to more or less steady swimming, while those loose horses plunged, snorted, and often made turns. (40–41)

While her parents fretted over the health of the oxen and the daily pace and size of the wagon train, Mary Ellen embraced her "strange new adventure" (21). Most days she would walk ten miles or more with nothing before her or behind her but the land and whatever it held. She noticed how the red birds of Kansas gave way to the owls and mockingbirds of Nebraska; how the fuller woods gradually thinned into the more sparsely scattered cottonwoods and poplars once her family of six reached the plains. Even the soil seemed to have more space in it, with its sandier, looser texture. She laughed at the prairie dogs' frenetic barking and gathered armloads of wildflowers that helped break up the monotonous lay of the land: bluebells, buttercups, purple and white lupine, blue fax (46). "Yes, sometimes our eyes did ache from looking out over the barren plains facing the evening sun, but when the sun was setting the whole expanse was glorious" (46). As a child she was able to live in the moment more easily than her parents, who carried their anxieties about every mile, every step of the way.

Both new life—bison, prairie chickens, Indians—and death were part of Mary Ellen's daily experience on her two-thousand-mile journey. In a way that might seem harsh today, this pioneering nine-year-old saw up close the way the prairie sun can bloat an oxen carcass, the stomach distended and taut, or the way cholera can move through the system of a healthy man or woman and drain the life out of them in a day. "In each case the patient would suddenly take violently ill, retching and purging, often lapsing into an unconscious state closely resembling death. Father feared that some might have been interred before they were claimed by death owing to the great anxiety to get out of the infected locality" (55–56).

The Todd family was less than halfway to Oregon when the two younger daughters—Louvina and Cynthia—became ill. The cause: "the murky unfit water of the Platte River. We tried to allow it time to settle before drinking" (54). Aware that a modern audience would shake a knowing finger, Mary Ellen defends her parents' ignorance. "Yes, of course, it would have been better if we had boiled it. You people now are much more clever in some ways, yet I do believe that we knew some things that many are now forgetting. I know my father could cure better ham meat, and mother could make better corn bread than any I ever tasted in these times" (54). But good corn bread could not save the two younger girls.

One day, just as we halted at noon, Louvina began suddenly to complain and soon was very ill, so we had to camp right there. As soon as possible father put up our tent some distance away. Then he put Louvina on a bed in it and told the rest of us to "keep out." Soon after, Cynthia turned pale, drooped her little head and soon was also sick. They cramped, chilled, and were deathly sick so that something must constantly be done in order to alleviate their distress.

John [her adopted brother, age sixteen] and I were left to see to the stock, keep up the fires, get water and keep plenty of it hot, also to help mother about the cooking and whatever was needed. (56)

Cynthia came back quickly but Louvina lay motionless for so long, the father called for a looking glass to see if he could catch the moisture from her breath on the reflecting surface.

"Did Louvina wet the mirror?"

"I think so, but we cannot know yet how it will turn out; we can only wait and pray."

[Singing] "Earth hath no sorrow that heaven cannot heal."

Coming to the opening of the tent, he said, "I believe your sister is breathing a little better. Won't you heat me some milk, adding a pinch of soda and bring it here?"

My feet fairly flew in doing his bidding. As I hastened to help mother prepare some toast, what did I care now if I did burn my fingers over the fire? Louvina was surely going to get well. (56)

The Todd's baby girls pulled through, but hundreds of other families on the trail that year did not experience their good fortune. Mary Ellen's family celebrated the Fourth of July by thanking God that they were not part of the procession of cholera and fever victims. By the end of the month both the parents and the eldest son of a family they were traveling with had died from Rocky Mountain spotted fever. "We often took the little five-year-old boy, Willie, who grieved so much for his mother, into our wagon, and tried to interest him. I tell you, those were bad times, requiring courage to keep up and going" (188).

By August Mary Ellen herself took ill with a fever and fell into a delirious state for days. Now every turn of the wheels sang out a harsh "Chugety Chug! Chugety Chug!" that tortured her aching body. At night she had visions of the dead Indians they had seen along the trail, who had fallen to smallpox. John had discovered a teepee stacked with dozens of bodies; inquisitive Mary Ellen had poked her head in only to recoil. And she relived in her mind an unsuccessful attack a band of Indians had made on their wagons.

I thought a young black-eyed Indian was throwing his lasso at me again, and I was screaming and trying to get into our wagon, but just could not. Then I heard father calling, "Honey, there is no one after you. Don't cry, Sis!" He then gave me a drink of water and bathed my face and hands. While gently stroking my head he hummed, "O Happy Day" until I began to feel more peaceful. I tell you my father was surely the best man in the world. He never lifted his voice in correcting any of us. He would merely say, "Mary Ellen, I believe you would better not do that." or "You do not want to grow up to be a selfish girl, do you?" He never had any trouble getting us to obey him. Nothing made me feel worse than to know I had displeased my father. (81)

She was not able to help much along the Idaho portion of the trail, but with each passing mile and every passing day, her strength returned. August gave way to September and a wet chill filled the night and early morning air. They would all bunch around the bonfires with their overcoats drawn tight. "Sometimes little Cynthia cried with cold hands and feet" (86).

The landscape awed Mary Ellen but rarely made her afraid, until her own father fell ill and her stepmother weakened after giving birth to a son, Elijah, on the trail. The boy just suddenly appears in the journal and the reader realizes that Angelina endured all the hardships of the journey while pregnant. The enormous land and enormous task of surviving closed in on Mary Ellen as she came to terms with her parents' vulnerability and her own responsibilities. Suddenly the voice of the girl who gathered flowers disappears in her account and an intense young woman takes her place.

Mary Ellen and her adopted brother John took "full charge of everything" (79). They listened to their father's fever-induced mutterings while they cooked mush with butter and molasses for their patients, milked the cow, collected firewood, gathered water, cleaned beddings, and led the animals out to some better grazing. In a manner reminiscent of a colonial-era girl, Mary Ellen shouldered an adult life. How she must have wanted to lean on her strong, reliable father and quiet, determined stepmother as she stood with her sunbonnet bending in the wind. The trail had already burned into her one unforgettable lesson: "People just have to help each other out" (79).

"That evening, [my father] seemed to feel a little better. John helped him to bed in the tent, and we tried to care for him as he had cared for us" (92). And when the small band of wagons reached the Cascade Mountains Todd had mad a full recovery. The four oxen, worn thin by the long miles and inconsistent diet, "had to pull and strain with all their might. We all walked over the worst places, mother and Louvina,

leading Cynthia and I carrying little Elijah. I just loved to carry the little fellow" (96).

Often going down the steep ridges proved harder than going up, so
the pioneers would thread chains along the mountainside. They would
hook their wagons to the links and try to control the pace of the de-
scent. But the sheer weight and sharpness of the incline made it a per-
ilous undertaking. Many a family saw all its possessions take a free fall
over some cliff. The Todds made it through, though their best oxen,
Buck, died at the bottom, overcome with exhaustion from the strain of
the downward journey. They had to use one of their milking cows as a
replacement in the four-oxen team.

A biting, steady rain sprayed down on them day after day as they
closed in on their final destination. At least the local woodland made it
possible to build decent fires. Mary Ellen savored the smell of the burning pine; the sappy scent was so much sweeter than the strong odors
that came from the buffalo chips or harsh brush they had been forced
to burn while in the dry lands.

Finally the family came upon the valley that had captured Abbott
Todd's imagination many months earlier while he lay yearning for
something new in Arkansas. "As we drew out more into the opening,
father halted the team, and coming back to the wagon, said, 'Praise the
Lord, we are through at last!' There was a moisture in mother's eyes,
but there was also a bright light shining there" (98).

Six months after leaving Mary Ellen's grandmother more than two
thousand miles back, the Todds made camp about twenty miles outside
of present-day Salem. The father read the 107th Psalm.

> O give thanks to the Lord for he is good;
> for his steadfast love endures forever!
> Let the redeemed of the Lord say so,
> whom he has redeemed from trouble
> and gathered in from the lands,
> from the east and from the west,
> from the north and from the south.
> Some wandered in desert wastes,
> finding no way to a city to dwell in;
> hungry and thirsty,
> their soul fainted within them.
> Then they cried to the Lord in their trouble,
> and he delivered them from their distress;
> he led them by a straight way,
> till they reached a city to dwell in.[3]

Abbott Todd sold two of his remaining oxen, which gave him enough cash to rent forty acres of land. He mortgaged the other oxen and worked splitting rails for hire to pay for the seed grain. That done, the family had one last journey ahead of them: the backbreaking task of building a home in a raw land.

In an effort to make ends meet, Abbott sliced so many rails he wore his hands down to the bone and had to be nursed by his young daughters. Mary Ellen saw her parents working relentlessly to build and prepare their new cabin before winter set in and she longed to help anyway she could. She kept herself busy spinning yarn, constructing cupboards and dressers out of boxes, and knitting stockings, which they sold for extra cash. "You see, we just had to keep the wolf from the door."[4]

Just after their arrival, Angelina asked Mary Ellen to clean all the primary cooking pans and utensils, like the ten-gallon brass kettle that had tarnished after all the heavy use on the trail. She hauled them all down to the spring and "scoured off all the signs of that long journey" (101) using sand, soap, and ashes.

Even though they were more settled now, hunger continued to gnaw at Mary Ellen. She rarely complained about anything during their trip, but time and again she drops comments in her journal that she longed for fruits and vegetables: "Oh for something green! I felt like saying, 'My kingdom for a head of cabbage!'" (92).

As it happened, their new neighbor in Oregon, Mr. McCorkle, had a large weed-choked potato patch that he had never bothered to harvest. Mary Ellen offered to do the dirty work if he let her family keep half the yield. She talked Louvina into joining her among the rank weeds.

His consent was gained and we went to work. It was hard to hunt out those dried vines and dig those little potatoes, among all those tall weeds, but I worked with a will, and got Louvina to pick up most of the potatoes. However, it was now winter time and the cold made our fingers sting. Louvina cried, so we took to making fires, that we might work awhile and then warm up for awhile. We kept on day after day until we had six sacks of those little potatoes for ourselves and six for the owner. We certainly were very proud of them and our folks were proud of us. (102)

Abbott rewarded them with some new books, and Angelina promised them some new dresses.

By Christmas the family had fallen into a less-harried routine. The girls went back to doing mostly domestic chores, such as knitting, sewing, cooking, washing, baby-sitting, and candle making. John went into the fields with his father and worked with the farm animals. Out on the prairie the girls had joined in many of the more manly duties, such as caring for the stock, but necessity had forced the family to break with convention. The parents seemed eager to get their girls back into fresh dresses and indoor activities.

But something must have grown inside of Mary Ellen as the power of her legs increased with each passing mile out there on the plains. Something about her sense of herself as a girl must have stretched and blinked as she foraged and roamed new territory after new territory with great success. All along the trail she could move in so many ways other than one step in front of the other.

By the time the Todd family had settled into their freshly built three-hundred-foot cabin in Happy Valley, Oregon, Mary Ellen was ready to explore how her father had got things going while on the trail. She was clearly not ready to emulate her stepmother's role as full-time indoor domestic.

Louvina and I still liked to play in our covered wagon, that, after its long, long journey, now was standing in our yard.

Occasionally all along our journey, I had tried to crack that big whip. Now while out at the wagon, we kept trying until I was fairly successful. How my heart bounded a few days later, when I chanced to hear father say to mother, "Do you know that Mary Ellen is beginning to crack the whip?" (103)

Mary Ellen finally had the physical power, and after months of watching her father, she certainly knew the form. What she had not grasped was that they were not on the trail anymore and the urgency and open spaces that had freed her had disappeared. In the more settled environs of Happy Valley, she was destined to a more conventional domestic life. "How [my heart] fell again, when mother replied, 'I'm afraid it isn't a very lady-like thing for a girl to do.' After this, while I felt a secret joy in being able to have a power to set things going, there was also some sense of shame over this new accomplishment" (103).

Mary Ellen still lived in a time in which her role as dutiful daughter took precedent over any personal agenda she might have. On the trail, she did what was necessary, which often pushed her into areas of work normally not visited by nine-year-old girls in mid-nineteenth-century America. The fact she could return to feminine labors indoors, such as cooking and child care, was a source of pride to her parents. It meant they had become settled enough to care about conventions again.

More than two million enslaved black children under age twenty lived in the United States by 1860, most of them born into bondage. Even though raising slave labor was the most profitable part of the plantation business, these children rarely received the food, clothing, and medical care necessary for them to survive. They died of diseases, such as tetanus and lockjaw, at four times the rate of their white counterparts.[1] If they managed to reach the age of ten, their life expectancy improved because they received more food once they took on an adult-size workload. As Wilma King points out, "Enslaved children had virtually no childhood because they entered the work place early and were more readily subjected to arbitrary plantation authority, punishments and separations. These experiences made them grow old before their time" (xx).

While Harriet and Louisa mainly worked as domestic servants, most slave children labored in the fields. They picked weeds, cotton, rice, and tobacco. They hauled wood, water, and prepared levees and dikes. After sunset their owners often put them to work making candles or doing laundry, both incredibly time-intensive activities in the nineteenth century.

Harriet Jacobs published her autobiography, Incidents in the Life of a Slave Girl, under the alias Linda Brent, first in America in 1861, and a year later in England under the title The Deeper Wrong. With remarkable candor she catalogs the horrors of her life and the life of her own daughter, Louisa. Time and again she makes it clear that they were valued only if they were useful, either as workers or as concubines. They were essential, but never loved or respected, which meant they gained nothing of value from their forced contributions. Only when they lived with each other and worked to improve their own lives as a family, does a sense of pride sneak into Harriet's writing.

HARRIET AND LOUISA
Oh Child! Thou Art a Little Slave

We were worked in all weather. It was never too hot or too cold; it could never rain, blow hail, or snow, too hard for us to work in the field. Work, work, work. [Frederick Douglass] (21)

Children till 10 years old to serve as nurses. From 10 to 16 the boys make nails; the girls spin. At age 16 go into the ground or learn trades. [Thomas Jefferson listing work assignments for slave children at Monticello] (23)

Most of the slave help worked in the tobacco fields, but Harriet Jacobs's father, Elijah, was a skilled carpenter, and her poised, intelligent mother, Delilah, was a domestic servant at the Horniblow's main house. During her baby years, the master's family allowed Harriet to live with her parents in a two-story wooden house in Edenton, North Carolina. She never saw her father whipped or overworked in the fields. Indeed, he was given tremendous freedom to go from job to job in the area. He paid his master a sizable percentage of his earnings, but he pocketed the rest. He bought his family's food, raised his own daughter and son, married and abided with his own wife, and tended to his own house like any other working man. "Though we were all slaves, I was so fondly shielded that I never dreamed I was a piece of merchandise."[2]

Then Harriet's mother died when Harriet was six. "For the first time, I learned, by the talk around me, that I was a slave" (3). In mid-nineteenth-century America six was considered old enough to polish brass, old enough to hold a fan over a southern white woman's wan expression, old enough to run up and down stairs at an acceptable pace, but not old enough to know in the fullest, darkest sense what it means for another human to own you.

I was told that my house was now to be with my mistress; and I found it a happy one. No toilsome or disagreeable duties were imposed upon me. My mistress was so kind to me that I was always glad to do her bidding and proud to labor for her as much as my young years would permit. I would sit by her side for hours sewing diligently, with a heart as free from care as that of any free-born white child. When she thought I was tired, she would send me out to run and jump; and away I bounded to gather berries or flowers to decorate her room. Those were happy days—too happy to last. The slave child had no thought for the morrow; but there came that blight, which too surely waits on every human being born to be chattel. (4)

Harriet's mistress died. The young girl drooped with grief—no more flowers to gather. Now both her mothers were dead. There was talk that the mistress had so cared for Harriet that she set her free in her will. At twelve Harriet must have had some sense of all that could mean to her life. Instead of wondering where they would place her next she could think about what she wanted to do. Unlike most slaves, Harriet had been taught to read and write. She could run a school. She could. . . .

After a brief period of suspense, the will of my mistress was read, and we learned that she had bequeathed me to her sister's daughter, a child of five-years-old. So vanished our hopes. My mistress had taught me the precepts of God's Word: "Thou shalt love thy neighbor as thyself. . . . Whatsoever ye would that men should do unto you, do ye even so unto them." But I was her slave, and I suppose she did not recognize me as her neighbor. I would give much to blot out from my memory that one great wrong. As a child, I loved my mistress; and, looking back on the happy days I spent with her, I try to think with less bitterness of this act of injustice. While I was with her, she taught me to read and spell; and for this privilege, which so rarely falls the lot of a slave, I bless her memory. (4–5)

When we [her brother, John, also went] entered our new home [owned and run by Dr. James Norcom] we encountered cold looks, cold words and cold treatment. On my narrow bed I moaned and wept. (6)

Harriet had reached a great divide, one that many children crossed in America when parents or masters valued them only for their net production. Until her move to Dr. Norcom's estate, the people in Harriet's life had valued her spirit and well-being. They cared that she took pride in her work and felt like a contributor. If things became too tedious, they let her roam. By today's standards, her hours of sewing and flower arranging seem harsh, but when measured against the life of the average young female slave, Harriet enjoyed a level of respect, love, and freedom that was rare in the South.

When she was given a linesy-woolsey dress, "a badge of slavery," and put to work for the mother of the young niece who had inherited her, Harriet ceased being a dutiful "adopted" daughter, ceased being a contributor, and became a cog in a machine—a replaceable part. The work may have been the same—cutting flowers, sewing—but the contract had changed utterly and with it Harriet's ability to gain pride and self-confidence from her labors.

No one cared if Harriet became weary from lack of sleep, too much work, or hours standing and waiting on the whims of her new owners. She no longer wove flowers into wreaths that she handed out as gifts to others in the household, because in the Norcoms' eyes she was not part of them. When her father died a year later, she was harvesting blossoms as decorations for the main house. None of those blooms wound up on his casket because the Norcoms refused to let Harriet break from her chores so she could pay her respects. They had a party to give. "I spent the day weaving them into festoons while the dead body of my father was lying within a mile of me" (6–7). When she pleaded to be released from her work, they chided her. Her father had spoiled her by allowing her to think she was no different than a white girl: "Blasphemous doctrine for a slave to teach; presumptuous in him" (7).

Down the road in a small house that smelled of homemade biscuits, there lived a free black woman who helped buffet Harriet from all the personal losses and horrible indignities of slave life: her grandmother. When she had gone to the auction block after the death of the mistress, a local white woman who considered herself a personal friend bought her for $50 then promptly set her free. Known as "Aunt Marty" to area folks, she supported herself on the sales of her famous crackers and jellies.

Because slaves at the Norcom farm where Harriet lived were expected to grab food whenever they could and were rarely given regular meals, the grandmother's kitchen became a crucial stopping point. "There was a grand big oven there that baked bread and nice things for the town, and we knew there was always a choice bit in store for us" (15). Those few moments breathing in the aromas of her grandmother's house must have been some of the freest moments of Harriet's early life. The thick smell in her nostrils, the special sensation that comes with knowing a piece of that is just for her. Oh, to carry that warm cracker in her hands as she trod the dirt road to her master's house. How it must have felt like a shield—something so completely hers she became almost teary eyed at the thought of eating it.

While her grandmother could supplement her granddaughter's meager diet—a problem so pervasive among slave children in the South that they died at four times the rate of white children—she could not block out the cruelty of life in the slaveholding town of Edenton.[3] At Christmas the slaves were given a rare few days off, but then the New Year ushered in "hiring day"; the day many of them found out what their work assignments would be for the year. "The slave is sure to know who is the most humane, or cruel master, within forty miles of him. It is easy to find out . . . who clothes and feeds his slaves well; for he is surrounded by a crowd, begging, 'Please, massa, hire me this year. I will work *very* hard, massa.'"[4] One hiring day, Harriet saw a woman lose all seven of her children to slave traders from New Orleans. "Gone! All gone!" she exclaimed to Harriet when they met in town. "Why *don't* God kill me?" (14).

A young girl absorbs the cruelty of her environment like body blows to the inner self. What must have broken inside of her as she watched a black man get beaten mercilessly because he dared to defend his wife against the sexual advances of the master? "I went into the work house the next morning and saw the cowhide still wet with blood and the boards all covered with gore. The poor man lived" (11). Strong men from her community brutalized into submission; strong women transformed into crazed handwringers. "Gone! All gone!"

Somehow the young Harriet managed to tap into the positive self her parents and other kind people in her life had helped her build and she used that like a reserve of honey. A laugh on the porch at her grandmother's house; a soft hour under an old cedar tree with her brother. She cherished these moments of human contact like an old woman near the close of her life. Harriet seemed to sense that even these meager offerings would fade as she closed in on puberty.

Hormones brought breasts, curves, changes that caught the eye of the middle-age Dr. Norcom. As the child of two mulatto parents, Harriet was a fair-skinned slave. Her brother managed to escape by passing himself off as a white man while onboard a boat to New York. As a girl, Harriet's skin tone was a ticket to sexual bondage, not freedom. Her complexion and education made her the perfect concubine—a piece of property with many of the features and social graces of a white woman.

After trailing her for more than a year with nothing to show for it but her growing hatred of him, Norcom began building a small cabin in a spot of woods several miles away from the main house. He planned to force Harriet to live there, away from the eyes of his wife and other prying neighbors.

My master met me at every turn, reminding me that I belonged to him, and swearing by heaven and earth that he would compel me to submit to him. If I went out for a breath of fresh air, after a day of unwearied toil, his footsteps dogged me. . . . The light heart which nature had given me became heavy with sad forebodings. The other slaves in my master's house noticed the change. Many of them pitied me; but none dared to ask the cause. They had no need to inquire. (28)

As Joan Brumberg explains in *The Body Project,* a more typical young teenage girl in mid-nineteenth-century America probably had not even begun menstruating yet.[5] While her duty to her family certainly entailed sexually responsible behavior, most daughters ages twelve to fourteen faced few temptations and knew far less than their media-saturated counterparts today. Church groups, sewing groups, parents, sisters, and other all-female networks policed and protected the emerging sexual selves of daughters in their communities. Many a fourteen-year-old girl knew absolutely nothing about sexual intercourse. The grand dame of the sewing circle was much more apt to focus a young girl's energies on mastering a dart or improving the consistency of her stitching.

Harriet lacked the protective net. Dr. Norcom's crude advances, not unlike the blunt content of movies, TV shows, and videos of today, forced Harriet to face a sexual dilemma she was ill prepared to meet both emotionally and physically. She loved her grandmother but feared her crushing judgment, so Harriet had nowhere to turn with her terrible predicament. While trying to navigate her way out of rape, she met a free black man, a carpenter like her father, who wanted to marry her. Norcom refused to sell Harriet, and the man went south to claim some land and start a new life. How the heat of that North Carolina summer must have closed in on the young woman as she watched her first love go and her own situation deteriorate.

I have told you that Dr. [Norcom's] persecutions and his wife's jealousy had given rise to some gossip in the neighborhood. Among others, it chanced that a white unmarried gentleman had obtained some knowledge of the circumstances in which I was placed. He knew my grandmother, and often spoke to me in the street. . . . He expressed a great deal of sympathy, and a wish to aid me. He constantly sought opportunities to see me, and wrote to me frequently. I was a poor slave girl, only fifteen-years-old.[6]

Harriet gave herself over to the eloquent gentlemen from town, Mr. Samuel Sawyer. "There is something akin to freedom in having a lover who has no control over you, except that which he gains by kindness and attachment. A master may treat you as rudely as he pleases, and you dare not speak; moreover, the wrong does not seem so great with an unmarried man" (59).

Perhaps the first time she made love with Mr. Sawyer, she had the same nervous anticipation any free girl has when she allows her newly minted sexual self to open wide. But Harriet was also a Bible-reading Christian raised in a social environment in which premarital sex was considered a brutish, horrible lapse. Her first pregnancy saved her from the cabin in the woods and Norcom's sordid advances, but it also exposed her to her grandmother's wrath. "'You are a disgrace to your dead mother.' She tore from my fingers my mother's wedding ring and her silver thimble. 'Go away!' she exclaimed, "and never come to my house again.' Her reproaches fell so hot and heavy, that they left me no chance to answer" (61–62).

Harriet fled, crushed by the only adult in her life who had done everything to strengthen and sustain her. She lay in shame on the floor of a neighbor's house, trembling and shaking for days. In the end, the early sexual experience proved more damaging to her self-esteem than the shift in the nature of her work and attitude of her mistress. Harriet felt she had no power over her situation, no way to get her bearings, no one to turn to for advice. Her sense of bewilderment—even terror—mirror in eerie fashion many of the emotional traumas and complaints girls talk about today because they get exposed to so much sex and violence at such a young age.

The grandmother listened in silence to her granddaughter's tale. "I told her I would bear anything and do anything, if in time I had hopes of obtaining her forgiveness. I begged of her to pity me. And she did. She did not say, 'I forgive you'; but she looked at me lovingly, with her eyes full of tears. She laid her old hand gently on my head and murmured, 'Poor child! Poor child!'" (62).

In 1829 Joseph Matilda was born, followed four years later by his sister Louisa Matilda. The pregnancies and Sawyer's attentions freed Harriet from her master's advances but not his rage. When Sawyer won the congressional election for his district, he headed to Washington, leaving his slave mistress behind with the two children. With the protector away, Norcom pounced and arranged to send Harriet and her children to the plantation to "be broken in." The children were his property because in the American South the mother's status determined the children's status. A slave mother could only have slave children.

"SLAVE MOTHER'S ADDRESS TO
HER INFANT CHILD"

Oh, child! thou art a little slave:
And all of thee that grows,
Will be another's weight of flesh—
But thine the weight of woes
Thou art a little slave, my child
And much I grieve and mourn
That to so dark a destiny
My lovely babe I've borne.[7]

As a house servant, Harriet had endured debilitating psychological abuse but had escaped the more physically brutal life of a field hand. Whippings, hot sun, cut hands, bent backs, caustic overseers—it was a life that took the life out of the most vigorous bodies. Children assigned to clear worms and bugs from the plants often wound up eating fistfuls of the insects if the overseer did not think they had done their job thoroughly. Many a boy or girl sat dirty, sweaty, starving, and exhausted in the three o'clock summer sun with nothing but worms to chew on. Even the strongest of young spirits faded away out there, and Harriet knew it.

Panicked by the prospect of seeing her children sent to the fields, she ran away. At first she hid in a friend's house, then the house of a sympathetic white woman, then the swamp. The bugs. The bugs. The terror of being discovered. The horror of knowing that "that man" still owned her children.

$300 REWARD! Ran away from the subscriber, an intelligent, bright, mulatto girl, named [Harriet], 21 years of age. Five feet four inches high. Dark eyes, and black hair inclined to curl; but it can be made straight. Has decayed spot on front tooth. She can read and write, and in all probability will try to get to the Free States. All persons are forbidden, under penalty of law, to harbor or employ said slave. $150 will be given to whoever takes her in the state and $300 if taken out of the state and delivered to me, or lodged in jail.[8]

In a rage Norcom jailed her uncle, brother, aunt, and her aunt's two children, including a two-year-old girl. For months he held them there, insisting they tell him Harriet's whereabouts, but she knew enough not to endanger others by sharing such knowledge, thus they had nothing to tell. Finally, desperate for the lost workers, Norcom let them out.

Rather than suffer the sight of Harriet's son and daughter, he decided to sell them south—any slave mother's worst fear. But Norcom failed to take into account Sawyer's own ties to his bastard children. Perhaps the congressman had a twang of conscience knowing that a boy and girl from his bloodline could become chattel for some sugarcane farmer. Perhaps not. Southern men who sired children with slave women often thought nothing of working their own kin as slaves and field hands. A drop of African blood and the whole family connection somehow got lost.

Whatever his motives, Sawyer finally decided to help. Working through a slave trader who never identified the buyer, Sawyer managed to dupe Norcom into selling Harriet's children to him—he bought his own children. Rather than suffer the consequences of having the boy and girl sent to Washington, D.C., where the congressman now lived with his new wife, he had them live with the grandmother. "Great was the joy in my grandmother's house! The curtains were closed, and the candles lighted. The happy grandmother cuddled the little ones to her bosom. They hugged her and kissed her and clapped their hands and shouted. She knelt down and poured forth one of her heartfelt prayers of thanksgiving to God. The father was present for a while" (120).

Harriet failed to find a ship or horse or safe road out of Edenton and wound up hiding in a nine-foot-long, but just three-foot-high, garret over her grandmother's house. Slave hunters had already searched the house and turned everything inside out. There was no reason for them to come again or to think Harriet would be fool enough to stay so close to her pursuers. Norcom was convinced she was already in New York City and spent the time and money to go there in search of her.

The air was stifling; the darkness total. A bed had been spread on the floor. I could sleep quite comfortably on one side; but the slope was so sudden that I could not turn on the other without hitting the roof. The rats and mice ran over my bed; but I was weary, and I slept such sleep as the wretched may, when a tempest has passed over them. Morning came. I knew it only by the noises I heard; for in my small den day and night were the same. I suffered for air even more than for light. But I was not comfortless. I heard the voices of my children. (128)

Six-year-old Joseph and two-year-old Louisa did not know where their mother had gone. One thing was clear: no one wanted to talk about it. A melancholy silence settled over Aunty Marty, who usually sang or chatted while she prepared her famous biscuits. When either of the children cried or tried to speak up, she told them to hush.

For the next five years, Louisa lived in Edenton, helping her grandmother by sweeping the kitchen, gathering firewood, and smiling sweetly at customers. Unlike her mother, she had no one to teach her how to read and write. As she matured into a young girl, she knew that something was amiss, but still no one volunteered any answers and she knew better than to ask. Aunty Marty was afraid her young grandchildren would prove forgetful and give their mother's presence away, so she kept it a secret and usually stole into the garret in the evenings with food for Harriet after the children were asleep.

Time and again Harriet thought she had an opportunity to flee, but something always came up: an unexpected patrol, a change in schedule, an unwilling boat captain. She began to lose strength in her legs, and her poor circulation left her chilled even in temperate weather. She feared she may become permanently crippled from the lack of movement.

Then even her daughter's voice was taken from her. At seven Louisa was considered old enough to provide some sort of domestic service, so her father sent for her to come to his residence in the Capital. In 1840 she made the long journey from Edenton to Washington, D.C.—the same journey her mother pined to take but could not because she did not have the necessary papers. Louisa met with an icy reception from her stepmother and mistress Lavinia Peyton Sawyer. In less than five months, Louisa was shipped off to Brooklyn to live with Mr. Sawyer's cousin, James Tredwell, a merchant. Lavinia probably found the young mulatto a painful reminder of her husband's past indiscretions (131–132).

Back in Edenton, Harriet spent whole days just thinking about when Lousia would write and what she might say. Just before she had left, Harriet had revealed herself to her, which had startled the young girl. It must have seemed strange to see the ghostlike image of her mother coming down from the deepest, darkest corner of the house. She had been only two years old when Harriet had gone into hiding, so Louisa had no memory of her face. Unlike her mother, Louisa could not write, so when she did finally send a letter off from Brooklyn, it was written by her new mistress: "[Louisa] is a nice little girl, and we shall like it to have her with us. My cousin, [Mr. Sawyer], has given her to me, to be my little waiting maid. I shall send her to school, and I hope some day she will write to you herself" (160).

The Tredwells never educated Louisa because they fell on hard times financially and could not afford to spare their young slave girl from her work. She could have attended a public school in Brooklyn for free, but they considered such use of her time an indulgence. They believed she was as educated as any slave need be.

Instead, nine-year-old Louisa spent most of her time running errands, such as fetching liquor for the heavy-drinking Mr. Tredwell or picking up cloth for sewing for the ladies of the household. Two years later when Harriet finally escaped by boat after seven brutal years in the garret, she sought out her daughter immediately. They met in the street but initially did not even recognize each other because the hard years had changed them so. "Signs of neglect could be discerned by eyes less observing than a mother's" (187). Even in the middle of their joyful reunion, Louisa was mindful of where her ultimate duty lay and told her mother she must hurry along on errands for Mrs. Tredwell. Harriet, all too aware of the slave–master relationship, encouraged her to move on.

Later, when they had more time to chat, Harriet asked her if she was well treated.

She answered yes; but there was no heartiness in the tone, and it seemed to me that she said it from an unwillingness to have me troubled on her account. Before she left me, she asked very earnestly, "Mother, when will you take me to live with you?" It made me sad to think that I could not give her a home till I went to work and earned the means. . . . [She] had been there two years, and was now nine-years-old and she scarcely knew her letters. (188)

The Tredwells also made it clear that they considered Louisa their property, though their claims were tenuous, since the father had put Harriet's grandmother's name on the bill of sale to protect himself. Harriet remained convinced that if she could support her daughter, she could take her away with her.

Harriet began working as a nanny and seamstress and had saved up $100 when she heard word that Mr. Tredwell had told the Norcom's where she was living. Once again, she had to flee. This time she meant to have her daughter with her. She pleaded with Tredwell's sister, who felt chagrined about her brother's betrayal so she agreed to release Louisa for ten days. The mother and child fled to Boston and never saw the Tredwells again. "She came to me clad in very thin garments, all outgrown, and with a school satchel on her arm, containing a few articles" (203).

For two glorious years Harriet, Louisa, and, at one point even her son Joseph, lived together as a free, self-supporting family. Joseph apprenticed to a tradesman and Louisa attended a local school. Then the other tradesman found out the fair-faced Joseph was actually a black man, and he had to quit. Desperate, he went to sea on a whaler and Harriet never saw him again. His disappearance made Harriet even more mindful of Louisa's vulnerability. Her daughter had to find a way to sustain herself.

Harriet's brother John, who worked for the Anti-Slavery Society in Rochester, New York, thought Louisa should attend a boarding school run by abolitionists in Clinton, New York. He offered to pay if Harriet could find it in her heart to let her child go. It proved a difficult choice for the fugitive slave after her seven isolating years in hiding and even more years on the run. Their tiny two-room apartment in Boston was the closest she had ever come as an adult to a home of her own. Without Louisa to fill it, it would seem little better than that lonesome garret. But Harriet also recognized how much her daughter would gain from having a decent education. It would set her apart from the millions of illiterate, poor blacks coming up from the South. Maybe she could even fulfill Harriet's own girlhood dream and become a teacher.

At the age of sixteen Louisa was one of three black girls to enroll in the Young Ladies Domestic Seminary, which was founded and administered by the famous abolitionist Hiriam Kellogg.[9] Initially her uncle paid the bills, but he had become disillusioned with the slow progress of antislavery legislation and took off for the gold mines of California. When the school learned her full story—that her mother was a fugitive slave and that she herself was in an ambiguous situation—they gave her a scholarship. At the end of four years she was fully trained as a teacher and more literate than her mother. When Harriet decided to publish her life story, Louisa copyedited the manuscript for her.[10]

Harriet never told her daughter anything about her father until the day Louisa readied to leave for Clinton. To Harriet's surprise, the young girl already knew the tale, as told to her by another servant in Sawyer's household.

I know all about it mother. I am nothing to my father, and he is nothing to me. All my love is for you. I was with him five months in Washington, and he never cared for me. He never spoke to me as he did to his little Fanny. I knew all the time he was my father, for Fanny's nurse told me so, but she said I must never tell any body, and I never did. (212)

Her mother had rescued her from the tobacco fields of North Carolina where she surely would have been beaten down as a common, illiterate field hand, whose only value to the plantation was the amount of tobacco she could pick and the number of babies she could bear. She escaped the disease and heavy workload that claimed the lives of so many slave children before they reached their tenth birthdays. Like her mother, she learned to read and write, skills probably less than 5 percent of slaves in America ever mastered. Yet despite these benefits, Louisa's childhood remained that of a girl enslaved by an indifferent family. They allotted her the barest amount of food, clothing, and education. Her biological mother did not live with her until she was eleven years old, and even then they had to endure the constant pressure that everything they had might be snatched away from them and Harriet would be sent back down South.

Both Louisa and Harriet had a few precious years as young girls helping out people who cared for them. But as soon as their household work became a service, not a contribution, it lost all power to build up and sustain them. They did not reenter a positive cycle again until they escaped and began a home of their own—a place where they were loved enough to play both giver and receiver again.

1861. Approximately 6.6 million children under the age of fourteen lived in the United States by 1861, accounting for approximately one-fifth of the total population.[1] When the country went to war, those living in the border states, such as Virginia and Maryland, saw the most carnage. All told 630,000 people died in the Civil War, half of them from disease.[2]

Mollie Gregory grew up in Alexandria, Virginia, a key city along the Potomac River in a border state that sided with 10 other Confederate States of America. Amid the stream of wounded and dying, the itinerant hustlers and armament of the invading Northern army, Mollie managed to live a relatively protected life. Her parents would have wanted her shielded from the day-to-day grit and grind even in the best of times, but to achieve that during the "War for Separation" was truly remarkable.

Time and again in her detailed accounts published in a newsletter put out by the historical society of Alexandria, Mollie makes it clear that she had few chores and almost no aspirations beyond being good. Out of the chaos of the Civil War, which completely undermined their Southern way of life, her parents managed to raise a coddled "modern" daughter, who was a modest contributor, at best, despite the demands of the times.

MOLLIE
A Romping Child

"In 1861 the war clouds hung heavily over Alexandria. The Stars and Bars were waving over the old town, easily in sight of the White House. Our boys were drilling on what the children called the 'Mustard' ground. We heard a cannon fire a salute when the state of Virginia seceded."[3] More than half of the residents of Mollie Gregory's river port town of twelve thousand fled the advancing Union army. Those who remained, like her parents William and Mary, and her younger sister Jessie, hunkered down in their homes, burying valuables in the dirt, hoarding food in the cellar and keeping as many things out of sight as possible. Mollie was charged with none of these chores, which were performed by house servants and adults, so everything still seemed quite distant to her: "War and rumors of war were nothing to nice little girls" (4:6).

Instead, she tucked herself away in a protective bubble. In 1861 she was a thirteen-year-old girl who liked to read, play with her paper dolls, and lounge in the garden that adjoined their home on Washington Street. When the Union army finally arrived, Mollie was in her pajamas.

One morning in May Emily, our maid, came in the nursery and cried out, "Get the children, the Yankees done come and took the town." We were dressed and on the pavement in time to see the U.S. troops coming down Washington Road. Our own boys were just leaving by way of Prince Street. Our married sisters, with their children, had gone to Culpepper Courthouse the day before. Belle and Julie (her older sisters) went with them, my father thinking to remove them out of any scene of strife, but like many others he believed the warlike situation would be over in a few weeks at most. These girls however were to be in the midst of bloodshed for the next four years. (4:22)

It is unclear why William Gregory decided to keep his two youngest girls—Mollie and Jessie, age eight—with him even though Alexandria had become an occupied town. In just a matter of weeks, northern Virginia's primary port, which competed with major cities such as New York and Baltimore, became a hushed version of its former self. The barber, blacksmith, tailor, watchmaker, dry-goods merchant, candy man, and many others fled. Hustlers took their place. These were people who knew no one in the community but had followed the troops with their collection of cheap trinkets. If the soldiers moved out, the hustlers moved with them.

Two young Southern girls must have seemed vulnerable in this stew of strangers and enlisted men, and yet William Gregory allowed his daughters to stay. Miss Ellen Mark had closed her girls' school at the start of the war, so Mollie did not even have classes to attend. "I was left pretty much to my own resources. At first I thought I would keep a journal, but soon tired of it, but being fond of reading, I found ample entertainment in our bookcases" (4:23).

Unlike many of her American predecessors and contemporaries, Mollie Gregory did not feel obliged to help with household chores or to make money knitting or sewing for the family. Her father had made a modest fortune importing and selling woolen goods from his native Scotland. By the time Mollie was five, he was already onto his second family and had enough stashed away to retire. Such stability translated into a childhood of complete leisure for Mollie. Not only did they have servants, in particular two slave girls—Eugenia and Sarah (both under age fifteen)—but several of Mollie's older half sisters from her father's first marriage also lived with them. When Mollie's seven-year-old brother Boyd died of meningitis in 1852, her half sisters nursed the mother through her grief. "Boyd's death nearly cost us the life of our Mother. Jessie was only a few weeks old and Mother lay unconscious for several days but finally returned to life. She always said that during that period she was conscious of something soothing happening every few minutes and when she aroused it was to find her loving step-daughters putting cool cloths on her head" (4:8). At the time Mollie was five, too young to play nurse to anyone other than her dolls.

Prior to the war, Mollie, Jessie, and sometimes Julie, spent most of their time under the shade trees in their yard. "We each had a garden of our own as well. I selected mine under a nice shady box bush where the industry of mud pie making flourished better than horticulture. . . . We often deserted our gardens and went down to the Potomac [River] to bathe at Old Point or Hampton" (4:7–8).

If they grew bored with that, there was always the main street, which brimmed with shops. They would press their faces against the window of Mrs. Apich's candy store, which had fresh lemon cakes, fragile cinnamon sticks, and jujube paste. Some days they even had a few cents to buy a treat or two. The braver souls skipped down the street to pull the bell at Aunt Airey's place. The old mulatto woman always came rushing out with a peculiar fury, as though half expecting an armed intruder. She would wave her curled taffy in each hand, scolding the children for making too much noise. Then she would huff back inside, leaving them there with their delicious prize.

Back home the slave girls Eugenia and Sarah, grandchildren to the woman who served Martha Washington at Mount Vernon, kept busy sewing, cleaning, polishing, waxing, and setting the table. Many of Mollie's older sisters seemed to engage in these activities from time to time as well, although largely so they could one day supervise like their mother. Mollie makes no mention of doing any domestic chores. The banks of the Potomac held her far tighter, especially on a humid summer day.

Mollie lived the life of the economically useless child, the trademark of a "modern" girl. Her skills were not essential to the well-being of the household. That left her free to be in the garden or down by the wharves where goods from all over the world got stacked high. Some afternoons she stood looking out her bedroom window, watching the pigs and cows that roamed through town. They often sheltered themselves from the sun or rain under the cedar trees outside her window. From that same perch she could watch for the man who came to light the street oil lamps on moonless nights. The faint glow of the flames gained strength as the twilight faded.[4]

During the summers, most of the family retired to a vacation house they called "Strathblane," which lay about ten miles west of Alexandria in Fairfax. Mollie and her sisters cooled themselves on the open porch or spent hours climbing the apple trees. At one point Mollie even made a tree fort and stuck a rocking chair up there. She would read and rock the hours away. The eighty-five acres offered lots of fine walking trails, which the children were allowed to explore as long as they took a dog along. "My father said 'Here the children could run wild.'"[5]

But when the Union soldiers took Alexandria, Mollie was cut off from Strathblane and most of the other comforting things in her life except her immediate family and home. No one could leave the city without a special pass and all Southerners were expected back in their houses by the 3 P.M. curfew.[6] Even when Miss Ellen Mark reopened her girls' school, which focused more on manners than their minds, things were not the same. Northern officers sent their girls there as well, which created a chasm within the class. "These were very nice girls but there was no intimacy between them and our southern children."[7]

No matter how much Mollie isolated herself, she must have noticed the thousands of wounded men that poured into Alexandria's makeshift hospitals. Every available church, warehouse, and old building was converted into a nursing station. Men from both sides of the conflict landed at this crucial crossing point along the river. Thousands of soldiers recuperated or died in Alexandria during the war.

Mollie must have also smelled the stench from the enormous slaughterhouses that sprang up on the west end of King Street to feed the Union's growing army or the aroma of bread drifting from the three-block-long federal bakery. Perhaps it was the relentless coming and going of the trains that she noticed the most, with their metal wheels striking the rails day and night, night and day, rat-tat-tatting with a sound like distant gunfire.[8] It was all there, but she mentions none of it in her personal accounts. Perhaps she just resented how much all the Union activities had taken from her. All the people she cared about were either gone or confined and headed nowhere, pinned down by curfews and special travel passes. Her own half brother was somewhere out on the front, working as a surgeon under General Hood's command.[9]

The only soldier she describes in any detail in her series of articles about her youth is a deserter who stumbled into her garden, desperate for some food and a place to hide his gun. "The Servants were off for their Sunday outing and we children were amusing ourselves with the kittens. The soldier had a gun which he asked to put under the steps. . . . I was going to put the musket in the attic and preserve it as a war trophy, but father directed John, our man servant, to take it down to the barracks" (4:32).

Even at fourteen, Mollie showed a remarkable lack of understanding about the hazards of the situation. At one point she made a few paper rebel flags for her father, who stuck them absentmindedly in his pocket. Fortunately, a neighbor spotted them before a Union patrol, and William Gregory quickly put them out of sight. "These children will surely get me into trouble" (4:32), he grumbled at the time, but there's no record that Mollie ever got reprimanded for any of her childish but potentially risky indiscretions.

Both of the Gregory girls became involved in the Knights of the Golden Circle, a collection of young women ages ten to sixteen who tried to raise money for the Southern cause by making knapsacks, clothes, badges, and rosettes to decorate baby clothes. The rosettes, in particular, were quite popular among the wives of the Union soldiers.[10] "Fancy articles were made and the smaller girls sent out to sell them to the wives of the Yankee officers, who were quartered around in the deserted homes of our friends who were refugees in the South. In the course of a year, our treasurer reported $128. This was turned into gold and sent South by a blockade runner."[11] And so the Northern invaders inadvertantly helped the Southern cause.

Mollie and her family felt duty bound to help the Southern cause, but when the war moved closer to home, their first charge was to protect themselves as a family. The Union army wanted all of Alexandria's citizens moved out of the area. The river port was just too vital to the Northern supply line, and they could not risk any antagonistic locals. "In the summer of 1862 most of the prominent citizens of Alexandria were ordered to vacate their homes and to appear on the wharf from whence a steamboat would take them to Fortress Monroe and then send them on to Richmond by flag of truce. This cruel order created the greatest dismay for many days as we all prepared for deportation" (4:24).

Actually both rich and poor alike were expected to leave, and many less prosperous families sold off all they owned for some desperately needed cash. The Gregory's were much luckier because a friend of the father's "appealed on his behalf to Secretary Stanton, who told him the order would not be carried out and that our father should quietly ignore it. The unhappy day arrived and we remained within closed doors, but peeped out of the shuttered windows as the sad procession went by, and we began to feel ashamed of our immunity" (4:24).

The family was spared the dicey experience of living in a town where they were exempted from the Union order while their neighbors were not, because Stanton did change his mind. "Soon the crowd came surging back and learned that at the last moment when the people began to embark a courier was seen galloping down King St. waving in his hand an order rescinding the former cruel one and allowing the southerners to return to their homes" (4:24).

The close call must have made Mollie's father have second thoughts about keeping his youngest daughters in Alexandria any longer. The awful diet and the constant threat of disease (Mollie, in fact, had fallen quite ill with typhoid fever and taken weeks to recover) made it clear that they had to go. By 1862 he no longer expected the war to be over in a matter of weeks, and neither his connections nor the walls of their garden could keep it out.

He arranged for Mollie to go to a boarding school in York, Pennsylvania, where an old Southern woman, Miss Sproule, had taken a number of orphan girls, "or the children of widowers who were in the Southern Army."[12] As Mollie headed out of town, she must have seen the field where thousands of prisoners of war lay without tents to protect them from the elements. She could not have missed the steady stream of wounded coming into the city and the hundreds of itinerant peddlers roaming King Street and Washington Street. After two years of watching the transformation of her hometown, she could no longer say, "War and rumors of war were nothing to nice little girls."[13]

She seemed to embrace her new situation at the school, if only for the better food and greater freedom.

I remained there until after the war was over, gaining in health and stature until when I arrived at home my brother William said, "I left her a rough, romping child and now she is a pretty young lady."

Miss Sproule had not been a very advanced up-to-date teacher but she surely knew how to look after the health of her girls and I fared better than I had at home where food conditions were bad. I had recently recovered from typhoid fever and was a slim, delicate girl; with very little information except what had been acquired from omnivorous reading. (4:33)

From her parents' perspective, she had what was necessary for a girl of her age: good health, good manners, and basic literacy. Nothing else was expected of her because she had little or nothing to prepare for other than marriage. When she did start her own household, it was assumed she would have slave help or hired help to do the basic domestic chores.

The war led to a boom in manufacturing that also dramatically altered the future for girls such as Mollie Gregory. Thanks to advances in production, they would grow up to run households that depended far more on store-bought goods. Instead of overseeing the production of spinning, sewing, shoemaking, butter churning, and other labor-intensive domestic duties, they simply purchased what they needed. That left them, and their daughters, with far fewer duties and a lot more leisure time. The question for families in the twentieth century would be how should they keep their girls busy now?

ADRIFT
1900–1941
Ethel, Amanda, and Connie

Be good. Dress properly. Help others. These were the words many girls lived by at the turn of the century. Daily life for most people had become less physical, thanks in large part to packaged foods, mass-produced clothing (sold through the Sears catalog, for example), and a general shift toward a more urban lifestyle. A young girl such as Ethel Spencer, growing up in a large well-to-do family outside of Pittsburgh, Pennsylvania, could race home from school with no concerns other than what game she wanted to play—Spider-Cow? Princess Irene? If she grew hot and thirsty, she drank from the cooler in the back. No pumping or hauling required. At night, before retiring, she was free to read by gaslight because her mother and hired helpers took charge of putting the younger siblings to bed. By 1900, where there was money there was generally idle daughters.

Because people's views on a college education for girls remained decidedly mixed, a real crisis developed among the well to do on how to keep their daughters busy. Ethel sank into a terrible depression because she spent her days after graduating high school teaching a Sunday school curriculum she did not believe in. As an unwed young woman at home with a mother who had servants, her options remained limited.

The Spencer daughters as a group reflect the huge change in attitudes toward higher education for girls between 1900 and 1920. When Ethel's oldest sister Adeline gave in to her mother's urgings and enrolled at Bryn Mawr College in Pennsylvania in 1905, she told no one and "never once confessed her shame to any man."[1] Less than a decade later, in 1914, one of the youngest Spencer girls, Elizabeth, went to Smith College in Northampton, Massachusetts, "without one rebellious murmur" (86). Emboldened by the easy acceptance of her baby sister's decision, Ethel finally matriculated at Radcliffe College in Cambridge, Massachusetts, in 1919, after years of floundering.

By 1920, most Americans had concluded that an advanced education was the safest solution to the idle hands problem. The notion began in the upper classes because they were more apt to have daughters with little to do; but within a generation it had trickled down and become a dream even an immigrant girl, such as Amanda, the Spencer's cook, might aspire to for her daughter. At the very least, immigrants pushed their daughters to finish high school because it dramatically improved their chances of getting a better-paying, white-collar clerical job. The dilemma always became whether a family could afford to lose a daughter's wages while she attended school. Amanda's could not.[2]

The shift toward more serious schooling for girls marked the second major break from an American culture centered on the home front. The first, of course, being the massive move into work outside the home. But most employed daughters, such as Lucy Larcom who worked in the Lowell mills, contributed their income to their families. Going to school reflected a fundamental change in attitude. It meant a girl could cost rather than make money, and could focus on her needs and future, not the demands of others.

But then the Depression hit and many a middle-class daughter found herself yanked back into the household economy. At first glance, this seems a disastrous step backward after all the strides made for girls in education, athletics, and jobs. Children such as Connie Sullivan, who grew up in a large middle-class family in Pawtucket, Rhode Island, in the 1930s, knew they could not afford to think of college when their parents struggled to pay the grocery bill. Public schools did offer sports, such as badminton or basketball (six to a side), but if there were family chores to be done, Connie skipped practice. In any given week, she felt lucky if she could make it to the official games.

But all of these new limitations, brought about in large part because of the family's financial straits, did not keep Connie and her parents from hoping and expecting that she would go to college. They did not cut off her participation in sports entirely. After all, she had a basketball team to try out for. And, in small ways, they opened up some opportunities for her. Desperate for help on their large newspaper route, Elizabeth and George Sullivan eventually let their second oldest daughter deliver papers with the boys, even though they considered it un-ladylike. Earning money from the route was more important than keeping up appearances.

The generation of girls who spent their childhood years—ages six to fourteen—struggling through the Depression wound up striding the fence between their roles as dutiful daughters working hard at home for the sake of the family's well-being and their lives as girls who could at least imagine opportunities in education and work that generations who grew up in the nineteenth century could not. They emerged from the other side of this tightrope walk the most productive, confident generation in American history.

Connie never had reason to doubt that she was anything but essential to her parents. She hung laundry, did dishes, watched babies in her family of nine kids, scrubbed floors, and performed an assortment of small errands for her exhausted mother. But all the in-house demands did not preclude out-of-house goals. Elizabeth and George Sullivan expected all of their children to attend college, even though they lacked the resources to pay tuition for any of them. Connie took advanced placement courses just like her brothers.

A glimpse into the Sullivan household in Pawtucket in the 1930s reveals a strong partnership between parents and children, one that focused on surviving a terrible time, but which also built dreamers and seekers. There was a tremendous process of give-and-take, with the overall integrity of the family—not any one individual—at the center.

1900–1914. The assassination of President William McKinley in 1901 ushered in a violent century of dramatic social and cultural change. Tucked away on a quiet side street on the outskirts of Pittsburgh, Pennsylvania, Ethel Spencer seemed beyond the reach of dead presidents, miner strikes, and immigrant slums, but they touched her life in a subtle fashion. Her father, who worked as a seller for the steel magnate Henry Clay Frick, arrived home each evening by trolley with his white shirt soiled by the soot that hung heavy in the city air. The Spencer family would then sit down to a dinner prepared by girls pulled from the Slavic slums on the south side.

In many ways the girls in the household most accurately reflected the great social shifts going on in America at the turn of the century. Amanda, the teenage immigrant hired to do most of the cooking, lived the duty-bound life of daughters of past generations. She labored hard in the kitchen all day and gave most of her wages to her father who worked in the mill. Her counterpart on Amberson Avenue, Ethel Spencer, had more freedom and more choices than just about any generation of girls in U.S. history. As a well-to-do white girl from established Protestant stock, Ethel was free to complete high school, explore other options besides marriage, and eventually secure a college education. Ethel lived the more modern youth that had previously been the prerogative of boys. She did not find her seven years off prior to college a fulfilling experience. The open-endedness of her situation actually frightened her.

After floundering around for many years, Ethel finally focused her energies on getting an advanced education and eventually taught English at Carnegie-Mellon University in Pittsburgh. In 1956 she wrote her memoir, The Spencers of Amberson Avenue, *which describes her youth in suburban Pittsburgh in the early 1900s, and shared copies of it with her immediate family. Two professors at the University of Pittsburgh felt the elegant account of her suburban life, when that social class was just emerging, was an invaluable historical artifact. In 1983 the University of Pittsburgh Press published Ethel's memoir, seventeen years after her death.*

ETHEL AND AMANDA
The Suburban Girl and the Cook

Ethel Spencer loved to ride in her grandfather's horse carriage with Old Dan straining between the shafts. He would clip-clop at a steady pace even on the bumpiest of Pittsburgh's roads, lulling her into a dreamy state. But on this particular day in 1900, eleven-year-old Ethel had another kind of ride in mind: Jimmy Reed's automobile. She and her brothers and sisters had camped out on the curb in front of their house on Amberson Avenue, hoping to catch his eye as he rattled by. "Nice boy that he was, he took pity on one little Spencer after another and invited us to share the high perch beside him."[1] Her seat quivered. The rush of dusty air stung her eyes as they drove down Amberson Avenue and then took a sharp left onto the soft asphalt of Castleman Street (8; map). Amid all the clatter, rush, and whirl, Jimmy somehow managed to keep his cap on. When he finally pulled over to let Ethel out, she raced for the house to share the big news with her mother and to gulp down some of the springwater stored in the kitchen[2] (20). It felt great to wash away the grit with such coolness, although the image of the ride stuck in her mind. Nothing in her life would ever wash it away.

That evening after supper Ethel's mother, Mary, retired to the library with her brood of seven and read aloud from Charles Dickens. "She read with enormous relish and with great dramatic skill" (73), while the children did their homework, sewed, or knitted. The drone of her mother's voice, the clicking of the needles, and the repetition of her own sewing finally quieted Ethel. By the time the chambermaid had lit the gas chandelier, the "motorcar girl" was ready for the big bed she shared with her sister Kate (11). The Spencers lived in a generous, four-story house in a well-to-do neighborhood, but with seven children, a live-in cook, chambermaid, aunt, and nurse or two, they needed every inch. All the children, except the oldest girl, Adeline, had to share a bed.

As a girl living in an industrial city at the turn of the century in America, Ethel strode the line between a nineteenth- and twentieth-century life. While she could catch a car ride with the boy across the street, she also had to come home to a house that relied on bottled water because the city system carried life-threatening diseases, such as typhoid fever. All of the daughters were expected to help their mother with the mounds of sewing required to keep their large family properly clothed, but they often escaped even this traditional chore because their mother paid for a seamstress to help her, bought the clothes at a store, or did the work herself.

When it became absolutely necessary, new clothes were supplied, but since no decent ready-made garments were available for girls, to get hold of what we needed was not easy. Even some of our underwear had to be made at home, and in consequence Mother spent much of her life at the sewing machine. . . . Every spring and every autumn, and often in between times, a seamstress arrived to get us ready for the coming season. (40–41)

Freed from one of their few chores, Ethel and her four sisters were just as apt to spend their afternoons chasing the ice wagon as stitching.

All the children would gather about the ice man as he broke an enormous cake of ice with his pick into pieces of a size to fit into refrigerators. We watched with admiration his feats of strength as he lifted up huge chunks with his tongs and carried them into the house. The minute his back was turned we began to scrabble about with the chips of ice at the open end of the wagon, trying to find pieces the right size for our mouths. When the ice man returned and drove away, there was always a fringe of children hanging to the back of the wagon. (67)

The ice man. The meat man. The farmer's market on Saturdays. Ethel's house on Amberson Avenue lay in a new neighborhood on the east side of Pittsburgh called "Shadyside" that retained a bucolic mood long after the heavy steel and iron furnaces had turned the old portions of the city into a sooty, urban landscape. Dozens of children lived in the area—the McClintocks, the Edwards, the Macbeths (59)—and played freely in the streets and local yards. Ethel's house became a favorite stopping point because her mother gave the children free rein during the day, while most of the other mothers confined their children to the nursery. "Perhaps it was because we had to be repressed in the evenings when our nervous father was at home that she allowed us to tear all over the house by day." The kids spent hours making up games such as Spider-Cow and Princess Irene (62). When it rained or they grew bored with outdoor play, they scrambled around the roomy corridors, cooking real food on the gas stove in the third floor toy room or dressing up in Grandmother Spencer's old clothes, the favorite being a gray tea gown that "had a trailing train that we liked to swish behind us" (66).

The "nervous father," Charles Spencer, made this cloistered life possible for his children by working as a sales agent for Henry Clay Frick, the coal king of Pittsburgh.[2] As the biggest local owner and supplier of a vital fuel, Frick seemed the ideal partner for Andrew Carnegie's booming steel operation. The two men eventually had a falling out, but not before Frick had a hand in making Carnegie Steel one of the most prominent and profitable companies in the world.

Charles landed his white-collar position in part because his wife's father, Judge Acheson, did what he could to make sure his son-in-law became something more than a shopkeeper. Frick proved a brutal overseer at every level, not just with the unskilled laborers in his mills. Many an evening Charles Spencer came home on the electric trolley to his Queen Anne–style house, his shirt soiled from the sooty air in the city and his head pounding from the relentless ten-hour day, and all he wanted was silence. One of the few expectations Mary Spencer had of her children was that they play with great reserve as soon as their father came home. Ethel makes almost no mention of her father in her memoir. She recognized his tense personality but never explored the causes.

By cutting herself off from her father's world, Ethel further isolated herself from Pittsburgh's dominate culture: the men working in the glass, steel, and iron factories that lined the three great rivers: the Monongahela, Allegheny, and Ohio. By 1900 immigrants and first-generation Americans made up nearly two-thirds of the city's population, which had tripled in size to 670,000 in just thirty years.[3] Most of them labored for wages so low that their wives had to take in boarders or take on domestic service jobs just so they could eat and live in a two-room shack. The intense heat of the furnaces, the twelve-hour workdays, and the poor diet took the life spirit out of even the best of them. For these Polish, Slavic, German, Italian, and Irish families, Amberson Avenue was a universe away from the Pittsburgh they had come to know and grapple with.[4]

Oddly enough young immigrant girls bridged the gap better than any other group. Households like the Spencers, with a large number of children and more than a dozen rooms to attend to, relied on the labor of black women and young teens just off the boat from Europe to run their households. And so it was that Amanda, a sixteen-year-old girl fresh from the borderland between Germany and Poland, arrived at 719 Amberson Avenue in 1904. Somehow she had found out about the job opening for a cook that the Spencers had advertised in the local paper.[5]

Ethel's memoir is full of the names of domestic help that came and went: Minnie, Bertha, Augusta, Anna. Her mother would train them, use them, and then "sadly lose them to husbands eager to take over such jewels" (30). Newcomers with language and cooking skills were a rare commodity in places like Polish Hill and South Side.

Amanda arrived too shy to go to the front door. "A big overgrown girl of sixteen, she was so fresh from the old country that she had to be accompanied by a child interpreter. Though she had no references, Mother, liking her substantial build and plaintive eyes, took her anyway and never for a moment regretted having done so" (33). Bertha Tretow, the German chambermaid, was not as charitable and looked askance at this brown-eyed Pole. The new girl could not speak a word of English.

At first Amanda had to communicate with her new employer through sign language. If Mrs. Spencer needed a chicken she would put her hands under her arms and flap about like a bird, then point to the cellar. Amanda always returned triumphantly with the chicken. "The problem of communication between Mother and her new cook soon ceased to exist, for Amanda learned quickly. In the early days she followed Mother about like a faithful dog, watching her every move. She would pick up each bowl and spoon the minute it ceased to be needed and say, 'Washen dis, Missus?'" (34).

For her diligence she received room, board, and $1.50 a week. To Amanda's father, who had made the Atlantic crossing with her, that extra income proved the difference. As a common laborer at one of the mills, Ethel's memoir does not say which, he probably earned about $10 a week, but he and Amanda needed a minimum of $12 a week for room and board. By living and working with the Spencers, Amanda made it possible for her father to save so he could eventually send for his wife.

She also escaped the living conditions of the working-class neighborhoods. As Poles, she and her father probably initially settled in Polish Hill or South Side (again Ethel does not say), which sat within walking distance of the mills (xxi). Night after night the flames from the Bessemer converters used in the steel-making process cast their light on the river. Perhaps those living in the nearby clapboard shacks found something soothing or beautiful in the flashing patterns, but a terrible process lay at the heart of the visual display. The water in the area was unusable and the air was so thick with soot and stink that, as one local newspaper columnist put it, it "smelled like Hell with the lid off."

With no running water, women had to go back and forth to the community pump several times a day. Washing their family's clothes in that filthy environment was an all-consuming task. To make ends meet, many of them even took in boarders, which meant even more dishes and laundry. Their husbands often worked twelve-hour days, seven days a week, which left any domestic chores, including cooking, the household budget, and child care, completely up to the wife or daughter.[6]

At 719 Amberson Avenue, Amanda lived on the third floor in a small room that had a washstand, a view of the surrounding neighborhood, and clean breezes. "But there was no bathroom." The servants had to "fetch water from a housemaid's closet on the second floor. Their toilet was a dark hole under the cellar stairs, and there was no bathtub for them anywhere. If they bathed at all, it must have been in the laundry tubs. There was nothing usual about these arrangements; our house offered as much comfort to servants as most others."[7] The tenement housing in areas like South Side often had community privies, so Amanda probably did not consider her setup a hardship.[8]

And so each morning, before first light, Amanda splashed cold water on her face and hands and headed for the plain kitchen. She got the gas stove going and took the dough she had set out the night before and kneaded it with her young, thick fingers. A dash of flour on the board to prevent sticking and then push and pull, push and pull. Into the pan and into the oven. "When the bread began to bake, the house was filled with a delectable fragrance. Only the taste of the crisp brown crusts themselves, thickly spread with good butter, was better than that lovely smell."[9]

Amanda's day soon became part of Ethel's day: the smells from her labors, the finished food on the table, the sound of the heavily accented girlish voice in the hallways. But a great distance remained between them despite their closeness in age. Ethel might learn something of cooking and shopping from her mother but those "lessons" were more like treasured personal exchanges than job training. At the farmer's market, Ethel would watch as her mother went about eyeing rolls of butter. Mary Spencer would take up an end of the paper in which a roll was wrapped, nipping off with it a bit of butter, tasting it appraisingly with rapid smacking of the lips, and as a rule rejecting it. A country woman with a good pound of butter one week was just as likely as not to bring in a bad one the next week, so the tasting ritual had to be gone through with every Saturday. The buying of chickens was just as ritualistic, though here it was a question of the breast bone. If the end of that bone was still flexible, the chicken was young, but it had to be fat as well as youthful. (21)

Ethel did not seem to think it her duty to master these skills for the sake of her future household. Perhaps she could see that the local supermarket, with its expanding selection of prepackaged goods, would soon make such knowledge obsolete. More likely she simply went along for the intimacy, not the training. Her immigrant counterpart, however, had to master the art of measuring flour for bread or risk losing her job.

While Amanda labored in the kitchen, Ethel attended the local public high school, where her mother expected her to work hard at "producing herself." That meant good manners, good grades, and music and dance lessons. While Amanda kneaded, Ethel studied. After school all the Spencers were free to play. They had few assigned chores and plenty of leeway to roam the neighborhood with friends. At the close of her ten- to twelve-hour day, Amanda retired to her small space on the third floor and studied English until she fell asleep (24).

Working-class families did everything they could to free their daughters so they could attend the local high school. Sons could apprentice in a variety of trades, but a girl who wanted to aspire to something more than domestic work had to have a high school education. The degree opened up doors for her in the booming white-collar sector and in teaching.[10] In the end, most families simply could not afford to give their daughters up, even for a free education. That precious $1.50 in additional income proved too essential.

Ethel's family faced a different set of dilemmas when it came to her education. Her mother had gone to college, a rarity for that generation, and had notions that her own daughters should do the same. The father thought such an expense a waste and preferred investing the money so they could have "income to live on in idleness. . . . For daughters growing up in the twentieth century, however, [Father's] was not a wise point of view. . . . Mother wanted me to go, insisted on my taking the college preparatory course at school, and hoped against hope that when the time came money could be found to send me."[11] The disagreement between the parents left Ethel enough room to feel she had a choice rather than an obligation to attend college, and she chose not to go. She had seen how her eldest sister, Adeline, who had given in to her mother's pleadings, had been afraid to say she attended Bryn Mawr College, because "it damned oneself in the eyes of all right-thinking males. She never once confessed her shame to any man" (82).

So Ethel stayed at home and taught Sunday school, even though she considered herself an atheist. She had hated the one unremitting duty that her mother had imposed on all the Spencer children: church services at the Shadyside Presbyterian Church. "Nothing but illness ever kept us at home on Sundays" (81–82). They squirmed and protested to no avail. They listened to a minister who expected them "to take a fare designed for adults and endure it" (93). After several hours at the main service, the children then herded into Sunday school classes, where they were taught "by maiden ladies of what seemed to us advanced years, or by young girls who knew nothing" (95). To her horror, Ethel had become one of those young girls who taught Sunday school simply because they did not know what else to do.

Around the same age that Ethel turned her back on college, Amanda made some key decisions of her own. She and her father had managed to save enough for her mother's passage to America, and sent the ticket off "triumphantly." All those hours of frying meats, kneading dough, baking over the stove even on the sootiest of summer days, and, finally, her mother would come. But then a letter arrived. "When she opened it, out dropped a piece of her mother's shroud. I can still see the look of grief in her brown eyes and hear her plaintive voice as she told us of her mother's death" (94).

The sturdy peasant girl that Mary Spencer hired in 1904 began to falter. Weakened by the terrible news, Amanda came down with typhoid fever and had to stay behind when the Spencer family went to the beach for its annual summer holiday. They made sure their cook had good care and left her with Dr. Klein. "Before we got home Mother received a letter from her, written, we thought by Mr. Klein himself, for Amanda's English was not yet equal to such elegance of style. In it she announced that she was going to marry Mr. Klein, who had been 'so good to me when I in hospital bed did lie'" (95). Amanda made a rare leap out of her class. Most immigrants married other immigrants (34). But thanks in part to her own hard work and Mrs. Spencer's guidance, she had become one of those rare jewels who knew how to cook, clean, and speak English. In just three years, she had come off the boat from Europe and jumped into a middle-class American life.

Ethel had more choices, which, initially, left her feeling bewildered. "The accepted pattern for girls in our youth was to finish [high] school, 'come out,' get married, and live happily ever after. For a girl who was not a social success, and did not get married, who had neither society, a husband, a house, nor children to occupy her, life was dull and meaningless" (34). But within the Spencer's own household, there were signs that a girl could begin to measure her life in a wider variety of ways. By the time Elizabeth, six years younger than Ethel, went to college in 1914 "college was a much more usual next step than it had been for her older sisters. She went to Smith without one rebellious murmur" (34).

For seven unhappy years, Ethel sewed clothes and taught Sunday school. "I could not teach with conviction, but it was expected that from my own profound ignorance I should enlighten a class of little girls and I lacked the courage to rebel" (84). But as Elizabeth's easy step into college life showed, going on for higher education was no longer seen as a radical step for a well-to-do daughter. Ethel had waited so long, she no longer needed the courage to be different, she just needed the money.

Her father had died in 1912, which left Mary Spencer with six of her seven children still at home. She sold some land on Amberson Avenue and cut a lot of the household staff, so she could save her pennies for her children's education. What was so remarkable about Mary Spencer is that she economized so she could send all of her children, not just her two sons, to college. In the end, as Ethel recalled in her memoir, "to her no sacrifice was too great if it won for her children the education she was convinced they needed to cope with life in the Twentieth Century" (86). In 1919, Mary's third oldest daughter Ethel, enrolled in Radcliffe College. She escaped "futility" and returned to the great task of "producing herself" (84). For an American daughter at the turn of the century that no longer meant simply marrying well.

1931–1941. As the symbolic heart of industrial America, Pawtucket, Rhode Island, is as good a place as any to explore home life during the Depression. Sam Slater first put the town on the map in 1793 by establishing the first mechanized mill on U.S. soil, a step that most historians mark as the beginning of the Industrial Revolution here. Over the years various manufacturers came and went, drawn by the areas three powerful rivers and labor pool.

The Depression put a major dent in the town's success story, closing down a host of companies and forcing many others to operate at less-than-full capacity. By the time the Sullivans arrived in 1931, nearly 20 percent of the local men were either out of work or involved in some sort of government-subsidized project. But Pawtucket remained a town with some jobs precisely because it was not a one-company town. All sorts of products, from thread to glossy paper, were made there.[1]

When it comes to the 1930s, most of us think of families forced off farms in the Midwest, but Connie Sullivan represents a more accurate take on the average child of the Depression. Her father had a job. They had a house and food. But like all of the other families that were just getting by, Connie and her parents were all too aware of how close to the line they lived. A sizable minority—nearly one-third of the population—could not even afford something as simple as the radio in the Sullivan's living room.[2]

In a manner reminiscent of Mary Ellen Todd on the Oregon Trail, Connie Sullivan had to step up. As the second oldest in a family of nine, much was expected of her and much was given. In a series of letters and personal interviews, Connie discussed her childhood in Rhode Island and what it meant to pull her weight on the home front even as she aspired to a college education.

1931–1941

CONNIE
I Had 78 Pennies

The two porcelain-faced dolls lay hidden in a nook on the front porch, the fabric from their fine dresses showing slightly. A person would only see them if they knew to look, which Connie Sullivan, age five, and her sister Shirley, age six, did not. Christmas was coming and the girls' mother had stashed the dolls there for safekeeping. But December brings cold nights in Holyoke, Massachusetts, and the porcelain cheeks cracked in the freezing temperatures.

Connie remembers "Mother crying on Christmas Eve. I was so upset that Mother was crying. Dad just said, 'Leave her alone.' Christmas morning Shirley and I got our dolls with the cracked faces, but we thought Santa had dropped them. I loved that beautiful bruised doll. Mother loved dolls. We all made clothes for them."

For several years in the mid-1920s, the Sullivan girls had few chores, porcelain dolls, and a large lawn to roll around on. "I know Mother and Daddy were a happy, young married couple. Dad owned a paper company and his fierce, independent nature was satisfied. He was a dapper, successful young man and Mother was a beautiful young woman with two babies to love." Even when the babies kept coming—first Shirley in 1922, then Connie in 1924, then three boys in three years—the center held. The father, George Sullivan, a chemical engineer and entrepreneur, had built up a prosperous company, thanks in part to the economic boom that followed World War I. The Sullivans owed nothing, lived well and worked hard. And despite the national craze to invest in the Great Bull Market in 1928 and 1929, George Sullivan stayed out. He preferred calculated risks—investments that he had a hand in and could control, like the paper company he co-owned with two other men.

But millions of other Americans had different investment plans. They bought up land in California or Florida and built thousands of homes, thinking people would come. At first they did, but not enough of them, so the banks called in the loans on the unsold homes and countless investors had to declare bankruptcy. Other Americans played the market with equal ignorance and when stock prices plummeted instead of rose, they panicked. The mass dumping of shares forced prices down even further. By Tuesday, October 29, 1929, the market had dropped $15 billion in value. By November, the leading industrial stocks in the United States had lost 40 percent of their value.[3]

George Sullivan did not lose money in the market, and he certainly did not own or build on any land in Florida or California, but all these forces conspired to put him out of business anyway. As more and more segments of the American fabric unraveled—hundreds of thousands of farms folded, real estate deals went bust, investors lost their capital, businesses experienced a dramatic drops in sales, the unemployment rate soared from 4 percent to 24 percent—the pinchers closed, and in 1929 alone nearly thirty thousand businesses folded, including George Sullivan's company.[4]

"1929. CRASH. Everyone's life changed. My life and relationship with Dad, and Mother and Dad's relationship to each other. . . . *Their world crumbled*." In a separate colored ink Connie wrote in her journal, "The crash was our family disaster. Dad had to go to a job he hated—he hated working for someone else—and Mother now had six children to handle in an atmosphere of stress and unhappiness. She went from a single home with help in a neighborhood she loved, to a three-family house and life with an unhappy, discouraged husband."

George Sullivan found work as a plant manager at the Blackstone Glazed Paper Company in Pawtucket and moved his family there. At the time, the unemployment rate for men in town was about 13 percent, with another 6 percent dependent on government work projects for their paychecks.[5] Nearly one-third of the city population received public assistance of some sort. George Sullivan knew he was lucky to have a job and a home for his growing family, but that did not change the fact that he had made up his mind to hate Pawtucket. It represented his lost business and, more important, his lost freedom.

His frustration boiled out in small ways. "Connie, get me a hammer," he barked as he tinkered with something outside their new home, a jam-packed three-family rental. She hurried inside but tripped in the doorway and twisted her ankle. Her slender hands grabbed at the pain as she hobbled into the downstairs den. A half hour later her parents found their auburn-haired, seven-year-old daughter rocking herself quietly.

"Constance, what are you doing in here?" her mother asked, before noticing her ankle, which had swollen to three times its natural size.

"Why didn't you just tell me?" her father said.

"I was afraid."

"Am I that bad?" he asked as he turned to his wife Elizabeth.

The new town made all the Sullivans edgy. With seventy thousand people, Pawtucket had more bustle, more industry, and certainly more strangers than Holyoke, Massachusetts.[6] The neighbor upstairs did not like children, which made their tight living quarters even more suffo-cating because Elizabeth Sullivan had to constantly worry about keep-ing things neat and quiet. But by 1932 her husband was secure enough in his new job to gamble on a higher rent—$9 a week—for a single-family home. Things would still be tight—the children slept three or more to a bed—but they had their own yard and no neighbor overhead.

For those with money, Pawtucket had a lot more to offer than Holyoke. The downtown of the mid-size New England city boasted a splendid movie theater, music hall, New York–style department store, ice cream parlor, and a grand public park. The Narragansett Race Track was a favorite weekend hangout for the locals who loved to bet on the horses.[7]

Because little Connie Sullivan had few pennies to spare, the new, more glamorous town did not necessarily represent a better world than the one she had known in Holyoke. While living in the old house, Con-nie sometimes looked after one of the babies by rocking it in the chair on the front porch, but she never minded because she could look out across their fine corner lot at the trees and sun. Then a friend might come by and she would be free to go and play where she pleased. In the evenings, she often held a skein of yarn, which her mother rolled into a ball while chattering away about her favorite movie stars. "My arms would get tired, but I loved having Mother to myself."

By 1933 Elizabeth Sullivan had no time to spare for her second old-est child. Two more babies had arrived during their first few years in Pawtucket, bringing the total number of children to eight. From time to time an out-of-work uncle lived with them, as well as a grandmother. At one point, George Sullivan was the sole provider for a household of thirteen. "Mother worked VERY hard and tried to give us as much free time as possible." But as the second oldest girl, Connie soon found herself saddled with a growing list of chores. There was little time to make play clothes for dolls now. Babies needed bathing, clothes needed washing, dishes needed cleaning, and vegetables needed canning. "Actually the canning didn't seem like a chore. I looked forward to working the grinder and having time with mother."

Young Connie would hook the grinder to the side of the wooden kitchen table, the screws turning easily in her slender hands. She would stuff a fat tomato in one end then watch, with glee, as it came out in pieces on the other end. The pulp of the tomato, the sweet paste of the red pepper, she loved all vegetables—except the onions, which made her cry.

Some days during the fall, with the winter season fast approaching, Elizabeth had several of her oldest children in the kitchen grinding away "until we thought our arms would fall off." They would all watch as their mother meticulously sanitized her jars, lids, and rubber seals. "She imprinted in my mind how absolutely essential it was that you did everything in a careful manner. You could get terribly sick if it wasn't done right. But never once in all the time mother canned did we have any problem."

Elizabeth had the water in the large pot boiling strong by the time all the jars were packed and ready to seal. Everything in her kitchen moved in smooth order, from the cleaning and crushing to the sterilizing. The steam wrapped its warm breath around the whole operation, fogging the windows and fringing Elizabeth's hair with a light dew.

The finished jars cooled for twelve hours or more on the counter in the kitchen. They were full of soft colors now—a slice of red here, a streak of green there. The following day Elizabeth and the children would carry the jars down to the basement, where they stood in rows like a collection of colored marbles. During the really lean years, the things they canned as a family made up the bulk of their diet, especially in the cold months. The salty bit of the diced tomatoes was a welcome alternative to butter.

By age nine one of Connie's other big jobs "was hanging out the wet laundry. Mother did not have a washing machine or dryer. One day I came home and hung out all the laundry with clothespins. Just as I finished, the line broke and everything fell to the ground. I rushed in crying. Mother just said, 'Calm down. Take the clothes off the line and take them to the basement. Rinse off the dirty ones. I'll call your father to buy a new clothesline.'"

Later that evening, a tired George Sullivan strung a new line, then went inside for dinner. Connie got sent out into the dark with the basket of clothes. This time she was alone with her aching arms. "I was tired. I have no idea when I had time to do my homework."

And yet her parents considered schoolwork a vital part of her day-to-day duties. All of the Sullivan children attended the local public schools and all of them followed the college preparatory track. The parents had no idea how they would pay for college for so many children, but they made it clear that when and if they had the money the boys *and* girls would go. With that in mind, the parents encouraged their kids to participate in sports, theater, music, the debate team, and whatever else the schools had to offer. But as the number of babies increased and the Depression deepened, the workload at home began to impinge more and more on school life, especially for the two older girls.

When Mother wasn't feeling well—she was carrying a child—she would keep Shirley and I home to iron. It took a whole day to iron for the family. I remember one day I really wanted to go to school. I was playing on the badminton team, but I had to stay home. Mother was so good, loved us so, and worked so hard, that when she was sick you just helped—never complained.

The kitchen table was stacked with dampened clothes, the ironing board was up, the kids had been sent off to school except for Tommy (age four) to watch. I cringed at the task ahead of me. About an hour later, the parish priest came in. He scolded me for being out of school. I looked at him and said, "My Mother is very sick in the bedroom. Please go in and see her." When he left, he just blessed me and said that he hoped I could go to school tomorrow.

Despite the personal and financial pressures in his life, by 1935 Connie's father had already begun laying plans for his escape from Pawtucket. Two nights a week he worked as a consultant for other paper companies in the area but asked to be paid in machine parts rather than cash. Piece by piece he was building his own printing press in the basement, which he planned to use to restart his business. Many an evening the Sullivan children heard their moody, driven father banging away downstairs. None of them so much as took a peek at what he was doing unless he told them to. They were too young to understand the pressure that was building inside him each day he worked for someone else. The frustration brewed and brewed and transformed the dapper, entrepreneur Connie had known in Holyoke into a quiet, tight, fierce man. It meant everything to him to break back into his former life.

Amid the tension and chores, the Sullivans found solace in the radio. They could afford a decent set and most evenings some or all of the family would sit around and listen to favorites such as *Amos 'n' Andy*, an enormously successful comedy. Many an evening George Sullivan would come home late, stash his latest piece of machinery in the basement, and then sit down to listen to the news. Connie would massage his scalp in silence. Elizabeth often came in to join them, and stayed to listen to one of her favorite variety shows, such as *Major Bowes' Amateur Hour.*

While all the children could listen to the radio, in general only the older girls went to the movies with their mother. Perhaps it was Elizabeth Sullivan's way of giving back to her daughters, who, because of their age and sex, wound up helping more around the house than the others. No matter how tight the family budget, the mother almost always found a way to pull together a few dimes to take in a show. The two sisters alternated weeks. To save money on the trolley, Connie and her mother would walk the mile down to the Leroy Theater, which had a full stage, plush seats, and a splendid balcony. They were not alone. Nationwide more than one hundred million people visited their local theaters every week during the 1930s. They went to see John Wayne on the big trail, Johnny Weissmuller in the jungle, or Fred Astaire and Ginger Rogers on the dance floor.[8] The lights would dim, the sound would rise, and everyone in the room would find themselves in a world very different from the one they dragged themselves through day after day. Elizabeth Sullivan could not get enough of the movies.

Connie's other favorite getaway was an outing with her best friend, ten-year-old Mildred Clark, who lived around the block. She would come by the Sullivan house many evenings and shout, "Mr. Sullivan, when can Connie come out?!" and he would often tell her his daughter had a few more chores to do. When she was ready to go, Connie's wire-thin frame would break out the front door and she would hop on Mildred's bike (she did not have one of her own), and they would ride down to Slater Park to feed the ducks or watch the carousel go round and round. "We never had the money to ride it, but it was fun to watch." In the summer, when the light held longer in the sky, they would spend hours down there.

"I never really felt overworked, except when mother was sick—just before and after having a baby. Mildred and I had lots of time together. Mother did a huge part of the chores. We lived in a nice neighborhood. I never felt poor, just that we didn't have enough money to buy extras. The poor couldn't afford a paper. We had a house, a radio, food, clothes."

By 1936 the whole family seemed to have turned a corner and Pawtucket had begun to feel a lot like a real home. The youngest Sullivan, Tommy, now five, could go to school in the mornings, which gave

Elizabeth some time for herself. The bigger kids were old enough now to help out in substantial ways and even contributed to the household financially by selling papers, blueberries, and tip sheets at the local racetrack. Everything they earned went into the household fund. But then the landlord raised the rent to $11 a week. Elizabeth, now pregnant with her ninth child, became hysterical.

I had never seen her so upset. I thought we would be out on the street. Dad tried to calm Mother. He said he would work two nights a week to make the extra money. I had nightmares of having to leave our home.

We stayed. Dad worked overtime, but money was tighter than ever. If we had holes in our shoes, we put in cardboard. Mother made a coat for Shirley out of Dad's old coat. We were lucky. Mother could sew like the wind. I wore Aunt Esther's old fur cape. I never complained, but I froze walking back and forth to school.

We had oatmeal for dinner. Sometimes mother would make just cupcakes and purposely leave them out so we'd spoil our dinner—because there was no dinner. We were told to tell Dad that we had all eaten. Mother saved meat for him. He always asked if the children were fed before he ate and Mother always said, "Yes."

At this point, an exhausted Elizabeth Sullivan could no longer carry the full load of the household herself so all the children had to step up. Unlike Mildred Clark's family, where the boys did just outside work and the girls did inside work, all the Sullivan children did all the chores, except sewing, which only the girls did. All of them worked to strip and make the beds, sweep the floors, clean the dishes, iron, hang laundry, and work outside jobs such as a newspaper route to bring in extra cash. Connie did have to conjole and argue with her parents for more than a year before she convinced them to let her ride the boys' bike to deliver newspapers. They thought it inappropriate for a girl to carry a heavy sack or to go up to strangers to collect money. But by 1937, at age thirteen, Connie had made her case and was assigned Sundays and most holidays. She would load up her sack, hop on her bike, and ride with the river breezes full in her face.

Riding the bike and yelling "Extra! Extra! Get your paper," I still remember the sheer joy I felt. I was happy as a child could possibly be. I charged 5 cents for a 3 cent paper. I went up three flights of stairs in a tenement to a gruff huge man with a jersey stretched over his belly and suspenders holding up his pants. He needed a shave. He bellowed I charged too much. He asked for the paper, and I said, "Give me 5 cents and I'll give you the paper." He gave me the money and I threw the paper between his legs and ran like the wind.

Not all the children were happy about doing chores normally assigned to the opposite sex. Connie's brother Richard, age ten in 1937, balked at doing the dishes. Girls' work! His mother told him if he could not wash the dishes he could not use them. For the entire day, every time he tried to use a plate or spoon or cup, his mother would grab it out of his hands. By dinner time he was ready to do his share.

Even for the girls, who knew such tasks were expected of them, the sheer volume of work could be overwhelming. One day when Connie returned home from school, she found dishes piled everywhere in the kitchen and pantry. Her pregnant mother was lying down too ill to get up.

She called out to me—she was heavy with child—and asked if I could please clean up. I kissed her and said yes and then went to the kitchen and stood there and cried. In time, I did the dishes, but I was exhausted. Never would I have told Mother I could not do them. That weekend, when Dad was out and Mother in bed, I was so sick of doing dishes I had each kid take a plate, eat his dinner, clean his plate and call the next kid. They ate one at a time using the same dish. No dishes to clean that night.

The Sullivans were not the only family struggling to get by in Pawtucket, which made it easier for them to accept their spare living conditions. Most of the people living around them were going through similar struggles or were even worse off. Conditions at many of the local factories became so intense—long hours, low wages—that the workers launched strikes. As a manager, George Sullivan came out on the side of the owners and talked the workers at his factory into backing down. He insisted that they would bankrupt the company with their demands and wind up with no jobs. Employees at the Blackstone Glazed Paper Company listened, but the situation in the textile mills was far more volatile.

Workers in the mills joined up with a nationwide effort, lead by the United Textile Workers Union of America, to improve conditions in the factories. At one point as many as five hundred thousand textile workers launched a strike in twenty-one states. As many as twenty thousand mill hands in the Pawtucket area refused to go to work. The Rhode Island State Guard came in to break up the demonstrations and killed two strikers. At one point the Guard even mounted machine guns near one of the plants. Several of the mills did go bankrupt, which just further increased the welfare rolls in Pawtucket. Many of the families left, hoping to find better luck in some other industrial town.[9]

The only thing Connie remembers of all of this is that her parents told her not to go down near the Leroy Theater for a while. Her father came home night after night in a state of complete exhaustion. She would massage his head, and they would listen to the news on the radio.

The increase in rent forced George Sullivan to take cash rather than machine parts for his consulting work, which stalled his dream of building his own press. There must have been days when he saw no way out. The tenseness in her parents affected Connie, who sensed their fragile state despite their outward show of strength. On the cold winter days when her mother gave her four cents to ride the trolley to school, Connie walked in her flimsy used coat and pocketed the money. The fear that one day her family might have nothing made her hoard every penny she could get her hands on.

"Constance. Do you have any money stashed away?" Once again Elizabeth Sullivan had no money for food, and she knew Connie had a habit of squirreling away pennies. "I hated to tell her," Connie wrote years later. "I had 78 pennies. It had taken me a year to save them. She hated to take them, but we had no money. 78 cents could buy quite a lot back then." The Sullivans had meat that week.

Despite the penny-pinching, the used clothes, and the meager diet, few of the Sullivans ever felt poor. When the eldest daughter, Shirley, accepted a charity food basket from the high school, her father marched it back in a rage and told them to give it to a family whose father did not have a job. "When people look back they see us as poor because they compare us with what you all have today. But back then hardly anyone had anything and we certainly had something."

A few hobo types would come by every week to the house on Clarner Street. We were told we could give them bread and water. This one time, I was about 10-years-old, a man came down the street and I was sitting on the steps. He stopped. Turning toward me, he said, "Do you think I might have a glass of water? Can I sit with you?"

"Oh, yes," I said, and came out with water and bread and put something on the bread for him. We did a lot of canning and had some things.

He was such a gentleman. So soft spoken. Eyes so sad. He was clearly a highly intelligent man. We chatted for about an hour. I still remember his stooped back as he was walking away. I wanted to run after him and tell him I'd get him a job. So many capable people who did not get work. I always wondered what happened to him.

In 1937 another recession hit the country, but things actually improved in the Sullivan household. The children were getting older and were able to work at more substantial jobs. Connie, now in high school, got work at the local Five and Dime two days a week. The boys continued the paper route, the girls baby-sat and sold tip sheets at the racetrack. Everything they earned went back into the household. George Sullivan's spirits improved because he felt with war looming that the economy would pick up and open the way for him to start his own business. He was right.

By 1940 George Sullivan had all the pieces he needed for his printing press and escaped Pawtucket. The blue-collar New England town that the Sullivans had moved to with dread had proven a good home for most of the children, but the father never learned to like the place. He went to Springfield, Massachusetts, on his own, where he rented a small room and found some free space for his press in the bottom floor of another business. He did their printing at no cost in exchange for the office. Back in Pawtucket, Connie was finishing up her last year in high school, and her mother did not think it right to move her until she had finished. The education of each of the children remained a top priority, and even though they could barely afford it, the Sullivan's sent their oldest child, Shirley, to college in Boston.

A year later the rest of the family followed the father and moved to a rented farmhouse in the countryside of West Springfield. George Sullivan, who had spent his boyhood among the loggers of Maine, fetching water for them as they worked at pushing logs up the river, loved the outdoors. Nothing relaxed him more than to garden a few hours or to watch the sunlight pull away over a plowed field at the close of day. But his wife did not share in such joys and found her new isolation away from all her old friends and cherished theater stifling.

With the Sullivan Paper Company barely up and going, Connie knew she needed to earn a steady paycheck. She found full-time work at a Dutchland Farms Restaurant in Springfield as a short-order cook, but this time her parents let her keep some of her wages because she wanted to go to nursing school and needed to save for tuition. Meanwhile, her brothers and sisters went to school, spent at least an hour everyday working in the family's enormous vegetable garden, and helped around the house just as they had in Pawtucket. The older boys also helped out at the mill every day, where George Sullivan was running a press that, by law, required two men to run, but which he operated alone. The new business became the most important thing in the Sullivans' life. If the father needed help, the boys gave it without complaint. If they needed cash, the children gave what they had.

Once again I had saved my money up. And once again, Mother and Daddy needed it. There was this big conference up in New York that he needed to go to for new clients. They wanted me to loan them the money I had saved for school. I was horrified. The vision of the 78 cents that I never got back went through my head. But of course I said yes. They took all my money so I figured I just would not go to nursing school. I did not say anything. But when January rolled around, they paid my tuition. I do not know where they got the money.

We all worked together to survive. Mother and Daddy worked so hard, I never really wanted to complain.

Connie Sullivan was flipping burgers on the Dutchland Farms' grill, the jabber from the people in the restaurant rising in a din around her, when the news came over the radio: The Japanese had bombed Pearl Harbor.

I was 17-years-old. I'll always remember standing there over that grill and the sudden silence. You could hear a pin drop. Then everyone just got up and left. Most of them were thinking of the boys, not the girls. There had never been any women in the service.

When I got home Mother and Daddy were in the living room. Daddy was smoking a cigarette. They were concerned about Terri [the oldest boy], who was 16. They never once thought about the girls.

But two years later, with their parents in no position to pay for their college education, Connie and her sister Shirley joined the United States Navy. Their answer to "What to do?" reflected the balance they had learned to strike in their own lives between duty and personal fulfillment. Thanks to the G.I. Bill, they could free their parents of both the cost of their living expenses and their college education with one swift step. They could serve their country even as they opened up a host of new opportunities for themselves: life in a big city, job training, financial independence.

At first Elizabeth Sullivan was not convinced that what the family would save by way of expenses would offset what she would lose by way of help and companionship at home. The military seemed such an odd, even frightening, option for a girl anyway. But Connie and Shirley would not be denied. They knew the WAVEs would open windows for them they never thought possible and they were right.

LUCY LARCOM. Lucy was the epitome of the dutiful daughter, often at the expense of her own education and aspirations. Even though she worked ten-hour days in the textile mills from age eleven on, she carved out a writing life for herself and became an accomplished author in the 1850s. (Photo courtesy of the Peabody Essex Museum, Salem, Massachusetts.)

MARY ELLEN TODD. The rigors of life on the trail going West in the 1850s meant young daughters such as Mary Ellen Todd (seated far left) often took on physical chores normally delegated to sons. Once her family settled down in Oregon, however, Mary Ellen found herself once again assigned to indoor chores, the purview of most girls of her generation. (Photo courtesy of Ross Gedeborg.)

MARY ELLEN TODD. As a young mother on an isolated ranch in Idaho, Mary Ellen (seated here with her first husband John and their child) needed all of the skills her parents had taught her to survive as an adult out West. (Photo courtesy of Ross Gedeborg.)

Mary C. G. Powell

MOLLIE GREGORY (Mary C. G. Powell). Mollie's parents managed to shield their daughter from most of the horrors of the Civil War that raged around them in Alexandria, Virginia. Surrounded by slave help and elder sisters, Mollie (pictured here in her young teens) had few responsibilities other than to be good. "War and rumors of war were nothing to nice girls," she said in an article she left behind about her childhood. (Photo courtesy of Alexandria Library, Special Collections, Alexandria, Virginia.)

ETHEL SPENCER. Even in the fledgling suburbs of Pittsburgh, Pennsylvania, in 1900, most families sewed their own clothes. But Mary Spencer reflected the wave of the future: She did most of the needlework herself, hired outside help, or bought what she needed. Her three daughters, including Ethel (pictured here at age nine in her favorite dress) spent far more time playing than doing chores. (Photo courtesy of Anne Spencer.)

Happy Play Scene in Mary and Elizabeth's Room
October, 1903

ETHEL SPENCER. Less a baby-sitter and more just another child at play, Ethel Spencer, age fifteen (second from left), enjoyed considerable leisure on Amberson Avenue in Pittsburgh, Pennsylvania. (Photo courtesy of Elizabeth Ranney.)

CONNIE SULLIVAN. The demands of the Depression forced many parents to revert back to a domestic dynamic that saw children as vital contributors to the household economy. Connie, age twelve in this photo, often stayed home from school to do chores, such as laundry, for the family's nine children. When she earned money delivering newspapers, she gave her wages to her parents. (Photo courtesy of Constance Collins Cain.)

CONNIE SULLIVAN. George and Elizabeth Sullivan expected all of their children, boys and girls, to go to college, but after struggling through the Depression they did not have the cash to send even one. Connie (pictured here in her Navy WAVEs uniform at age twenty) and five of her siblings solved the problem by joining the military in 1944, which qualified them for money toward a college education under the G.I. Bill. (Photo courtesy of Constance Collins Cain.)

LYNN GENESKO. Lynn, a sensational teenage breaststroker in the early 1970s, was one of the first women to receive a full athletic scholarship to a Division I college program. But the wonderful breakthroughs in sports came with a price that we continue to see at every level for boys and girls today: The hyper-focus required of serious competitors leaves them little time for a role at home. (Photo courtesy of Lynn Magnusson.)

MEGGY, ALLY, AND SARAH HODGKINS. "We need to be tool givers to our children," says Cindy Hodgkins, mother of Sarah (top left) age seventeen, Ally (top right) age fourteen, and Meggy (left) age ten. Even though the girls attend a large public school in a major city, they remain remarkably untouched by drugs, eating disorders, teen pregnancy, and other problems that plague their counterparts nationwide. The secret according to their parents: The girls value their family roles as much as their personal goals. (Photos courtesy of Cindy Hodgkins.)

BACK HOME
1955
Tina and Beverly

The zip and independence that characterized many middle-class girls growing up between the turn of the century and World War II fizzled by the 1950s. Daughters continued to work after high school and attend college at record rates, but by the time they reached their early twenties, they pulled the hand brake on their own express and got married. Tired of all the disruptions caused by the Depression and the overseas battles, people wed and had babies in astounding numbers. It seemed everyone wanted to settle down, and in 1950s America that looked more and more like a mom at home full time with the children, while the dad went off to work.

The changes for mothers had a profound impact on daughters. Many of them found themselves in a suburban landscape where "every woman stayed alone in her house . . . like a coin in a safe," as Annie Dillard recalls in her memoir, *An American Childhood*.[1] That left girls like Annie feeling trapped because their mothers represented what society expected them to become.

Author Betty Friedan captured this national surge of angst on the home front in 1963 in her book *The Feminine Mystique*. She described a world in which "each suburban wife struggled alone. As she made the beds, shopped for groceries, matched slip cover materials, ate peanut butter sandwiches with her children . . . lay beside her husband at night, she was afraid to ask herself the silent question, 'Is this all?'"[2]

Friedan received thousands of letters from women desperate to tell her about their struggles as homemakers or about their childhood's with at-home moms in the 1950s. "I hope one day, when my daughter is older—that she will read this book, even if out of curiosity—perhaps she will understand enough that she will avoid becoming a miserable housewife!" exclaimed a letter writer from Harrisburg, Pennsylvania. Another girl recounted the story of how a professor had asked her all-female college class what they wanted to do when they graduate. "No one seemed to want to be, or do, *anything*."[3]

The domestic life loomed darkly for so many of them because the very things that had made it challenging and fulfilling for past genera-tions had faded. The role of mother or daughter as manager of the household economy had given way to a much less engaging situation. Instead of orchestrating elaborate all-family canning sessions or har-vests, women and girls were picking up Campbell soup or Jolly Green Giant vegetables at the supermarket. And unlike their predecessors from the 1920s, few felt encouraged to use their newfound freedom to take advantage of opportunities in the workforce or education. Even the federal government got into the act of officially bullying them into going home by running ads that urged working women to give up their jobs to returning soldiers. Millions gave in to the pressure willingly, but others resisted and resented the shift in the social agenda.

By the mid-1950s, American culture had pushed mothers and daugh-ters firmly back into a service role. Those who broke the mold and took jobs often did so out of necessity and felt awkward, even embarrassed, about it. Little was available in terms of child care, so working moms often found themselves with the impossible task of handling a job, a household, and children.

Friedan pressed her readers to return to the spirit of the 1920s, when girls and women thought about careers and other interests beyond their role as daughters, mothers, and wives, but many writers wanted her to know that simply going to work was not the answer. "The vast majority of working women don't have careers," one woman wrote Friedan. "We have jobs, just like men. We work for money to buy things our families need. If we're lucky, we like our jobs, and find some satis-faction in doing them well, but it is hard to hold a commercial job, raise a family and keep a house." Another writer made it clear that until "men got some of their Victorian ideas out of their heads, then I am staying home. Unless he would be willing to help me with the housework then I cannot go to work" (ibid.).

Beverly Hill, a black girl who grew up in Los Angeles in the 1950s, had two full-time working parents, but unlike many of the women who wrote Friedan, Beverly's mom, Tina, loved her job as a skilled riveter for the aircraft manufacturer North American Aviation. The war left the Los Angeles area with a manpower shortage so severe that companies such as North American Aviation broke their own rules and hired not only women but also blacks. Tina knew that the miracle sequence of events that had landed her a skilled job that paid at least one-third more than what she earned cleaning houses was a once-in-a-lifetime break. She had gotten in and nothing, not even a new baby, could convince her to give up her job.

Beverly saw from an early age that her mother's job gave her power. If she wanted a new car, Tina bought it herself. If she wanted her daughter to have better shoes, she simply bought her some. Tina did most of the cooking, but her husband helped with the laundry and other chores. He respected and valued the fact that his wife had a job and realized he needed to step up on the home front.

Interestingly enough, though, neither parent expected much from Beverly. They had lived through chore-intensive childhoods on farms in Texas and felt flush with the idea that they could afford to free their daughter of all responsibilities. They saved for her college education and, despite their ten-hour workdays, rarely had her raise a hand around the house. However, because Beverly was a weak student, an only child with no clearly defined role at home, and a thirteen-year-old black girl in a predominantly white neighborhood, she struggled. Whatever benefits her mother seemed to gain from working a job she cared about paled when measured against the shame Beverly felt that her mother had to work at all. None of the white mothers had jobs. They certainly never wore pants the way Tina did. The 1950s culture pressed in on Beverly and made her feel as aimless and uncertain as any white girl growing up in a more conventional household. The fact that her parents represented the beginning of a whole new dynamic at home did not counteract society's larger message that a girl's primary role entailed little more than gliding through life until she married.

The 1950s as a whole represented a real throwback for most daughters. Especially among middle-class white girls, day-to-day life was no more demanding than the world in which Mollie lived in the 1860s in Alexandria, Virginia. Like Mollie, they were encouraged to make as few ripples as possible at every level of their lives. But unlike their nineteenth-century predecessors, they knew their generation represented a regression of sorts. In many instances their own mothers had taken jobs for the war effort or pursued higher education with a seriousness Mollie never could have fathomed. But when the war ended, everything contracted. The women went back home, often bitter about having to return full time to domestic work no one valued anymore. Their daughters felt the sense of loss, the closing of doors, and withdrew along with their mothers.

One writer, capturing the sense of disorientation that characterized many girls from this decade, told Friedan, "We are all sick, and most of us don't know it. And even if we know it, we can't figure out why" (ibid.). The cure, of course, lay in giving girls something that made them feel valued again—both at home and in the public arena.

1955. The 1950s was a decade of mixed signals for mothers and their daughters. On the one hand more girls were getting an education and moving into the workplace than ever before. On the other hand, American society as a whole made it clear that any woman who stayed on the job while raising a family was distinctly lower class. Pressured to marry at ever-younger ages, two out of three girls dropped out of college before graduating. Most were wed by age twenty and at least one-third had their first baby by that age, which marked a reversal of trends in American society since the 1920s.[1]

"They grew up and came of age in a time when new lives beckoned while prohibitions against exploring them multiplied" (11). This duplicity took firm root in the school systems, in particular, where girls and boys were often treated equally in the early grades, but then the issue of occupations would come into play and the girls would retreat into the background. Most of them understood that marriage and children lay in their future, while the boys sensed they must build a career outside the home.

As a black girl with a working mom, Beverly Hill is an excellent example of a young daughter caught in all of these cross breezes. Her mother takes pride in her work, but Beverly, influenced by the white middle-class culture that surrounds her, does not. Her parents value her education and try to downplay her domestic role, but Beverly does not excel in school and wants to sew and garden. Her parents' hard work wins her something her slave ancestors lacked—choice— but conflicting signals from society and her own parents make it difficult for her to take pride in the answers she arrives at as she tries to answer the question that every modern child must now address: *What should I do with my free time?*

1955

TINA AND BEVERLY
"I got sort of lost"

The master's wife gave Tina Hill's great-great-grandmother, Nancy, a glass bowl the day the former slave left the plantation for a new, freer life. According to family lore, the mistress told Nancy, "You're going to have to be keeping a house of your own, and I want you to have something that you're familiar with."[2] Today the bowl sits in a cabinet in Tina's home in Los Angeles. "That thing is over a hundred years old," she says. "It's been passed down from one family to the other. My great-grandmother gave it to her girl, which was my grandmother; my father was next, and then I'm next; then [my daughter] Beverly and then her little baby" (ibid.).

A quilting frame sits crammed in the corner of the cluttered dining room of the two-bedroom house, another reminder of the domestic history that ties Tina and Beverly to the black daughters in their past. So many of those young girls labored all day for white families then had to return home to do the same chores again in the evening for their own kin. Even as free women, Tina and Beverly's descendants toiled on the seventy-acre farm in Texas that the great-great-grandfather bought after the Civil War.

Tina's mother, Lucy, raised five children on the arid land after her husband died. The farm could not give them all they needed, so she also worked as a domestic for a white family in town. When asked if she helped her mother out much, Tina says no, but when pressed to describe her day-to-day life, she talks of mucking stalls, collecting eggs, weeding the garden, sewing, and helping her mother work a pressure cooker they borrowed every year from the 4–H Club so they could put up meat for the winter. These chores were such a part of the rhythm of her world, she did not see them as responsibilities, and pictures a completely carefree, barefoot girl when she looks back to that time in Texas in the 1930s.

Tina even found a way to flow in and out of the work her mother did for hire. "My mother worked for this lady so I just tagged along. A lot of times I did not go home. I slept right beside the fireplace at night to keep warm. Mama said I was just like she left me; when she'd come back the next morning, I would be right there."[3]

The entire family left the farm life when Lucy remarried and moved to a home in Prairie View, Texas, near the Negro Vocational College. Tina now filled her days with schoolwork, much of which had a practical bent such as sewing or cooking classes, but she did learn math, reading, and writing. In the end, not even literacy could free her from the fact that there were few opportunities for black women in the South, or anywhere in the United States in the 1940s. When she graduated from high school, she inherited her mother's legacy and took a job cleaning white people's houses.

Tina eventually escaped the low-wage world of domestic help by moving to Los Angeles just before the United States entered World War II. Desperate for military supplies, Great Britain and France flooded the fledgling aircraft and shipbuilding industries in California with orders. From 1938 to 1941, the number of people employed building planes in Los Angeles alone jumped from 16,000 to 120,000. Blacks began coming by the thousands, convinced they could get decent jobs in the fastest-growing region in the country.[4] Migrants such as Tina soon found that the companies had no intention of hiring minorities or women. For months, Tina had to resort to domestic work again at 60 cents an hour. But then the United States entered the war in 1942 and thousands of white male workers had to enlist. Suddenly even young black girls from Texas seemed employable. Earning $1 an hour, Tina went to work banging and patching "Billy Mitchell" bombers for North American Aviation. "Hitler was the one that got us out of the white folk's kitchen."[5]

By the time Tina married Joseph Hill and gave birth to Beverly, she had settled into her life as a working woman. She came from a long line of working mothers and saw no need to give up her hard-won position at North American Aviation. "We know the Negro woman was the first woman that left home to go to work," she says. "She's been working ever since, because she had to work beside her husband in slavery—against her will. She knows how to get out there and work. She has really pioneered the field."[6]

But while Tina was out in the workforce breaking new ground as a woman and a minority in a high-paying, skilled job, she took a very conventional approach when it came to raising her daughter Beverly, who lived the kind of circumscribed life typical of most middle-class girls of the 1950s. These well-to-do daughters were not breaking new ground; rather, they were moving back into old habits of uselessness on the home front.

Both of Beverly's parents worked hard as children and took pride in sparing their own girl the day-to-day grind so often imposed on black daughters in the past. Beverly did not have to collect eggs or sew her own clothes or watch other people's children. Her life could be like a white middle-class girl's life with days of free play. The only responsibility Beverly had around the house "was to stay out of trouble so my parents could go to work," she says. This proved an intimidating task since "trouble" to her mother and father could mean something as basic as borrowing her father's tweezers without asking. "I'd get a beating for that," she remarks, a touch of outrage still in her voice. She acknowledges that a lot of parents on their street beat their kids, but she felt hers were particularly quick tempered. The fact they both worked ten hours a day, five days a week certainly put a lot of strain on the household, but their exhaustion seemed to play less of a role in the overall pressure Beverly felt than their obsession with getting to their jobs no matter what. "Nothing was supposed to come between my mother and her job," Tina recalls, "Nothing. Each night she'd clean and iron her work clothes for the next day and lay them out. They both did that." If the school had some event parents had to attend during the day, the Hills never obliged. "They would not take time off for work for that; work was too important."[7]

As a young girl, Beverly did not know much about her mother's struggles as a domestic worker, her long days at the factory, and long years without promotions until she sued them for racial discrimination. "We did not talk about such things," she says, realizing in a way only an adult can just how brave and lonesome her mother's battle for fair wages and work must have been. To a ten-year-old, the intensity seemed intimidating. Beverly responded by withdrawing into herself. She became a skittish, quiet daughter.

Despite her fears and insecurities, Beverly managed to find joy in the hard-earned free space her parents carved for her. Most days, after attending her all-black elementary school, she would come home to her grandmother, who lived with them on Compton Avenue. "There were lots of friends in the neighborhood and older people who were at home. A girl lived next door," Beverly recalls. "We used to play Monopoly, checkers, dolls. They had all these new programs at the parks and my grandmother lived with us so I was not latchkey. I spent all day at the park, danced, played games, like shuffleboard, and performed in plays. There was just all blacks in these programs."

At the close of day her mother and father would come home and set to work in the kitchen crafting a full meal of home-baked bread, fresh meat, and homemade sauces. The Hills were not an affectionate or emotional family, so a luscious dinner was often the closest they came to an embrace. Despite her tired hands and eyes, Tina actually looked forward to the cooking as a way to unwind after an intense day.

Beverly remained outside the domestic work cycle and "never cooked a meal or cleaned the house." If she dropped clothes on the floor, Tina just picked them up. "I did not fuss at her, I just did it myself. All she had to do was go to bed and get up every day. My husband thought the sun rose and set on her and he did not mind cleaning her room. On Saturdays, we'd do the laundry together and he'd ask her if she needed a button sewed on or something like that."[8]

For generations on both sides of the family, daughters had taken on enormous amounts of domestic work, but in Los Angeles in the 1950s, with two solid wage earners in one family unit, a new dynamic emerged. An urban life meant no cows to milk or chickens to feed. More cash meant more store-bought clothes and food. A live-in grandparent meant another set of hands to do whatever light housework remained after Tina and Joseph hopped their morning bus. It had taken several generations, but Nancy, the slave, now had a descendent— a black daughter in America—who had absolutely no chores.

But like her white counterparts, Beverly was not sure what she was supposed to do with all her free time. She knew her mother had begun to save for her college education, but Beverly had no such aspirations. Words just floated on the page when she tried to read; numbers just jumbled around in her mind. After years at the same school, she had not bothered to find the library because she knew when she got there she would not be able to read anything. "I was one of those kids that the teachers did not pay attention to one way or another. I just was not important enough. I got sort of lost in the middle of things."[9] The teachers were slowed by huge class sizes, horrible supply shortages, old textbooks, and all the ills that came with being a school for blacks in a system run by whites.

Tina eventually put away more than $10,000 for her daughter's education, but she never spoke directly with her about going to college. She could see for herself that Beverly felt uncomfortable with schoolwork.

By 1955, American culture, in general, had few expectations when it came to advanced education for girls—black girls, in particular. If Beverly never finished school, she would be doing no more or less than what most people expected of her.

The only strong model in Beverly's life was her capable, employed mother. Beverly understood from an early age that it was her mother's job that gave the family a leg up on their neighbors. The extra income meant Beverly could have Buster Browns instead of black-and-white saddle shoes, lunch money when no one else could afford to pay cash for warm food, and trips to national parks where the astounding landscape broadened her mind more than anything she encountered in her segregated classroom. On Saturdays, they strolled down Central Avenue with other black families, but unlike most, frequently they went out to eat for their favorite gumbo. On Sundays, they bought bags of popcorn and roasted peanuts from street vendors, while the warm breezes of Los Angeles brushed their faces.

Even though they lived in an all-black neighborhood on the east side of Los Angeles, Beverly continued to see her mother's work in a positive light. At age ten, she could not see herself in college, and she did not help around the house, but she could imagine herself employed somewhere, perhaps in a skilled job like her mom's. Many of the other black families they knew had women that worked, though few saw the kind of paychecks Tina brought home from North American Aviation. As a welder and riveter she earned as much as her husband, who jumped from job to job, first as a pressman, then a janitor, and then to North American Aviation with his wife. Her income "gave her a voice. It gave her power," says Beverly. "She could do things, make choices. She never had to depend on my father for money for a car so she chose her own car. She outsaved him."

Then in 1958, they moved. The Hills were doing so well financially that they decided to leave their black community for a more upscale white community on the west side of town. The neighbors had greeted the first few blacks that moved there with burning crosses and threats, but the Hills went anyway. Tina and Joseph had the cash for a better house and they were going to use it.

For the first time Beverly was immersed in white middle-class culture. Things that once filled her with pride began to fill her with horror. "My mother wore pants to work, not pretty dresses. Over in the east, if you worked at the post office, you had a good job, but over there in the west, if you worked at the aircraft company, that was a low job." To most white suburbanites in the 1950s, a working mother was an aberration, a sign of trouble—the reason why Beverly struggled in school. To Beverly's chagrin, Tina made no effort to fit in. "When she picked me up at school, she'd be wearing pants and she'd cuss the teachers out if she was unhappy about something. She did not speak the King's English. I did not see these differences on the other side, but saw them here."

Financially, the Hills held even with their neighbors, but Beverly knew that did not amount to anything. People around her scoffed at the fact that her mother had to work to help them sustain their standard of living. What Beverly did not know was that many of these same people, especially the women and girls, were going through a crisis of sorts, precisely because they lacked the opportunities that Tina had made for herself. They felt incapable of working, of aspiring, of buying a car on their own.

Many of the letters that women wrote to Betty Friedan after she published *The Feminine Mystique* reflect a deep disgust with the restrictions placed on their lives and mothers' lives both at home and in the workplace. A thirteen-year-old white girl penned a letter thick with anger about her mother, who left her teaching job after she got married so she could be at home full time "Before getting married, she was a teacher; my father has always been a factory worker. My mother's IQ is high; my father's low. What hell it must be for an intelligent, ambitious woman to try to live through an unintelligent, unambitious man! But that's precisely what she has been trying to do for all of these years."[10] As for the girl herself, she excelled at school, but no one—not even her parents—thought that commendable. "I really enjoy studying—that's the shame of it. I'm unfeminine. I try not to like studying so much and never admit to anyone my real interests because I'm so afraid of being unpopular." Her parents opposed sending her to college "because girls do not need it" (ibid.).

By the time she was thirteen and living on the west side, Beverly had a much stronger role model for a mother than the letter writer and most of her other white counterparts, but that could not undo years of having no responsibilities at home, no expectations at school, and, now, a culture that scorned Tina's way of life. Disoriented, unhappy, and unfocused, Beverly began channeling her energies into sewing. The quilting frame in the dining room remained a mainstay throughout her childhood, a place where she and her mother gathered, chatted, and worked together. The soft sound of a needle popping the fabric punctuated their conversations.

As a young girl Tina had learned to sew from her grandmother. When the elder woman died, Tina—then age nine—"decided I was going to do my best to excel at the things she did. I was going to keep those things alive. I learned to crochet. I love that, and I love to sew."[11] Of course, on the small farm in Texas, whatever clothes the daughters could sew for themselves were essential, while in Los Angeles the handiwork was merely an outlet, but that did not make the end product any less valuable in Tina's eyes.

Beverly loved the precision of the stitching, the color combinations of thread and cloth, the special time with her busy mother, and the crisp finished product. When her mother had her join the 4-H Club to keep her busy after school, Beverly did not mind that she was the only black girl. "I did not make close friends with the girls. I was not the kind of black child who wanted to be with them. I did not have a fit about it."[12] She simply sewed her way to acceptance. At every fair and festival she won some sort of prize for her work. By the time she was seventeen, she was running a business sewing bridesmaid's dresses and other elaborate projects.

But she did not stop at sewing. For years she had seen her mother tend a garden in their backyard. It contained narcissus and jonquils that were offshoots of flowers her great-great-grandmother had taken off the plantation the same day she received her bowl from the master's wife. Tina had brought them up from Texas and tended them in the California sun. Under the guidance of the 4-H Club, Beverly began building on her mother's garden and even started a chicken coop in the backyard. The very chores that Tina had escaped when she left her life in Texas became a starting point for Beverly. Unlike her ancestors who worked the land, sewed, cooked, and cleaned often under duress and in a state of complete exhaustion, Beverly could take to her tasks at leisure and for the simple love of executing a skill.

All her life Tina had done necessary things. Her mother needed her help on the farm. As a single woman in Los Angeles she had to have a job. When she finally had a daughter of her own, she freed her of as many obligations as possible but in so doing undermined her self-worth. When Beverly also failed in school—the one area in which her parents expected her to perform—she simply withdrew into herself.

All her childhood Beverly "never had to do anything." Eventually, she saw she could choose to do something and give her own life meaning. Faced with a culture that kept pushing girls toward a domestic life rather than a career or job, Beverly found strength in the very "duties" her mother had tried to free herself and her daughter from. Beverly's childhood offers a splendid example of what can happen when all of the responsibilities that tie daughters to their past are cut off. In an effort to shield Beverly from all that was oppressive about life for black girls, Tina lost sight of what was good about raising a daughter who felt like a contributor.

Section Four

REACHING OUT AND AWAY
1965–2000
Lynn, Meggy, Ally, and Sarah

The girls of the 1950s who grew up to become the moms of the 1960s saw enough rending of the social fabric to know things could change on every level—even the feminine. Emboldened by successes, such as the passage of Title IX, which prohibited discrimination on the basis of sex in any program that received federal money, parents began pushing their girls outward in earnest, and society responded in kind by providing ever greater opportunities for them, especially in sports.

At first things did not change as rapidly as Title IX advocates had expected because no one enforced the new law with any kind of consistency.[1] Officially, by 1972, Lynn Genesko, a champion athlete from Woodbridge, New Jersey, had as much right as a boy to join a track or swim team her freshman year in high school. But, first, the town had to come up with the cash for the new coaches and equipment, and more than one girl had to show she wanted to get involved.

Title IX also could not flip entrenched attitudes off like a switch. After resorting to training on a regional team located forty-five minutes from her house, Lynn won the state championship in the 100-meter breast-stroke. Her hometown newspaper gave the losing high school football team the big headline and relegated Lynn's story to the inside pages.[2]

But irate women continued to pepper the courts with lawsuits, which, in general, they won. Schools began to realize that while no one had come knocking to scold them for giving their girls' programs half the money allocated to the boys', they would eventually face sanctions if they did not take some steps toward equality.

Title IX proved imprecise and imperfect, but highly effective over the long haul. By Lynn's senior year, still there was no girls' swim team at her high school, but the environment had altered enough at the college level that she received one of the first full athletic scholarships offered to a woman by a Division I college.

When girls walked through the portal onto the field of highly competitive sports, it had a domino effect. If they could develop muscles, work with teammates, and strive for goals on the field, then they could aspire to more serious things on every level from education to work. The advances in sports became like a barometer for gains everywhere.

By the 1980s, nearly everyone agreed that athletic girls were more self-confident, better students, and in better health than their more sedate counterparts. The gains had been so immense that by the 1990s parents embraced sports as the ultimate solution to the "daughter dilemma." Families thought nothing of centering their entire personal lives around the soccer schedule of one twelve-year-old daughter skilled enough to make a travel team.

Today, parents' expectations for their daughters focus almost entirely on achievements outside the home. Most mothers would be hard-pressed to list chores for their children that went much beyond walking the dog or doing the dishes on occasion. Even more disturbing, girls and boys increasingly find themselves freed from all family obligations, not just housework. A soccer star skips an aunt's wedding so he can go to a big tournament. A sister insists on swimming the summer circuit, even if that means the rest of the family cannot take a summer vacation. A younger sibling spends most of her afternoons as a child watching her sister train, even though she makes it clear she hates going to her meets by crying and vomiting in the backseat of the car. As adults, the two women no longer speak to each other.

Generations of girls have fought for the right to achieve in ways their brothers do, but today far too many of these middle-class kids only know how to reach out and away. They obsess about their various successes without a thought for how their personal agenda fits into their family's life as a whole. And their parents indulge their destructive self-absorption because they think a win on the field will keep everything steady.

Cindy and Ken Hodgkins know better than to leave their daughters—and themselves—standing on such a brittle foundation. Like the Sullivans, they encourage their three girls to participate in sports and other extracurricular activities, but also like their Depression-era counterparts, they expect such outside activities to take a backseat to family obligations when necessary. Everything they do has to somehow enhance the connections they have to each other.[3]

If Meggy, Ally, and Sarah Hodgkins want to play soccer, their dad coaches their teams so they can arrange to have games at staggered times on the same field. One girl does not get to be involved at the expense of another. In the summer, when many of the girls' friends go to intense soccer camps, the Hodgkins leave for Maine, where they visit relatives and spend the entire month of August just doing things as a family. At home, the television gets shut off during the week to prevent squabbling. Internet access is severely limited and their computer is used mainly as a mail system to correspond with cousins in Maine. All of the girls do set chores such as cleaning their rooms, washing the dishes as a team, and walking the family's new puppy.

As the Hodgkins show, to build confident girls today parents must first and foremost make them commit to a home life. With today's modern stores and technology, that no longer means spending hours canning vegetables or sewing the family linens. It comes down to fostering a mind-set that encourages aspirations that respect the family dynamic.

What better way to make girls feel essential than to tell them they cannot go to practice today because they have to attend a relative's funeral? What is needed are small everyday steps that make daughters feel that their presence is vital at home, even if just on an emotional level. Forcing them to balance their outside activities with their domestic life is a strong place to start. It shows we care enough to want them home again.

1965–1972. When Congress passed Title IX in 1972, a piece of legislation that prohibited discrimination on the basis of sex in any educational program or activity that received federal funds, no one expected the law to serve as a catalyst for change in women sports. It was designed to give women equal access to educational programs. But young women, frustrated by the inequities in college athletic departments, quickly realized the new law could give them great leverage in court. If the men's soccer team had a budget of $100,000 and four coaches, then, according to Title IX, the women's field hockey team could demand the same thing.[1]

Since most universities received federal funding through their student financial aid programs, on paper it looked as though they had to comply. In fact the federal government proved slow about enforcing the new law, and the women's programs were conflicted about following in the footsteps of the hard-charging, over-hyped Division I men's teams. Was parity really a good thing? A large number of women in the field felt not. In the end some of their fears would be borne out as universities got around the need to give both departments equal funds by creating just one athletic department. Inevitably, the male athletic director got the top job, so the number of women heading up their own sports programs dropped dramatically in the 1970s (ibid.).

Such damaging shifts aside, Title IX eventually opened up all sorts of positive avenues for girls at every level of school, including college, where the top teams began to realize they had to start offering elite female athletes scholarships as well if they hoped to build competitive teams. Lynn Genesko, a nationally ranked breaststroker from New Jersey in the early 1970s, was one of the first women to receive a full sports scholarship to a Division I college. Her tale of training, competition, neglect, and success reflects all that is good and bad about the sports culture that people like her helped spearhead and that took firm hold among both sexes by the 1980s.

LYNN
The Sports Star

The pool water, thick with too much chlorine, stung Lynn Genesko's eyes and gave her long hair a starchy feel. No one wore goggles in 1964, especially not nine-year-old girls entered in some local club meet. She pressed her eyelids down hard to squeeze some of the water out, and just kept flaying away. At five feet and more than one hundred pounds, she filled her lane with a motion and weight most parents would associate with a boy her age. She won easily.[2]

But it was not until Lynn saw the Olympic swimmers on television standing on podiums with medals in hand that she decided to make the pool her life. Until then she had been something of a tomboy, who played with the local boys in the parks near her house on Lyman Avenue in Woodbridge, New Jersey. One day they all might play baseball, the next, tag football. But after seeing the swimmers she decided she wanted to "join" the Olympic team. "I told her you do not exactly 'join' it," her mother Lillian says.[3]

So her father, a sports enthusiast, began driving thirty miles to Rutgers University, where the coach there had started a swim program for girls age eight to seventeen. At first Lynn only went two or three times a week and swam about an hour or two each visit. She remained busy with school and general family responsibilities such as changing the diapers of her new baby sister Caroline. On Saturdays, her mother expected her to help clean the house, and during the week she had to do the dishes and other odd chores. "I recall early having to take up and hang out the laundry. I was always part of household activities. When my dad had to change the oil, I handed him the can."[4]

But even during this less hectic time of Lynn's childhood, her parents did not expect too much of her on the home front. Both the mother and father worked full time, an unusual situation for a family living on Lyman Avenue in the 1960s, but that did not translate into more responsibilities for Lynn. As a latchkey kid, Lynn wandered Woodbridge a lot on her own. "About once a week I would take a bus to the end of the line and meet my dad and he would go get his hair cut. I was only six or seven so I was very much on my own." During first and second grade she walked more than a mile every day by herself to her aunt's candy shop. "She let me pick out one piece of candy. I remember sitting among the comic books and the glass-front boxes with all those candies in them." By third grade she had switched to a school closer to her own house and spent most of her afternoons at the local park with neighborhood friends.

Baby Caroline, ten years her sister's junior, spent her days at a sitter's house. Child care was hard to come by for working mothers in the 1960s. Often the best option was just another mother willing to take a child into her own home for a fee. One hundred years earlier, Lillian probably would have expected Lynn to care for the newborn, but by 1964 few middle-class daughters took on such demanding duties. "I never saw Lynn as a primary caretaker for this child," Lillian says. "I guess I just wanted to be supermom. I felt it was my job to take care of everything. I had to clean the house when I was a kid and my mom relied on me to baby-sit. So I was used to taking care of the house. I felt Lynn could have some responsibilities—manageable ones—but certainly not taking care of a baby. I did not think that would be fair to her. She was ten years old when she began to take a real interest in swimming and I felt that was important."

Unlike Connie Sullivan growing up in Pawtucket, Rhode Island, in the 1930s, Lynn was not expected to place the needs of the household over her outside interests. Her freedom to choose her own direction each day sprang out of her mother's more restrained childhood. Lillian's parents never valued her education and made it clear that whatever money they could save for college would go toward her brother's schooling. She was expected to help out as needed at home until she got married and took charge of her own household. There was never any time for frivolous activities such as sports or drama classes. Her parents made it clear that the only thing she might aspire to outside the home was work as a nurse or teacher.

But Lillian would listen to none of it. If she could not go to college then she wanted a job in the newest, trendiest field she could find.

Good at math, she landed an entry-level position in a company working on the early stages of the modern computer. When she married an out-of-town boy from Perth Amboy, New Jersey, she still went back to work. When she had her first baby at age twenty-two, she returned to her job. "I accepted it because it was what she wanted to do," says her husband, Frank. So she stayed in the programming field full time right through the childhood's of her three daughters, who were born over an eighteen-year period.

Lynn picked up on her mother's determined pursuit of her work and her father's intense interest in sports and forged a focus of her own: swimming. The trips to Rutgers University became more frequent—as often as five times a week. "The whole family wrapped it's life around my swimming." Little Caroline, still a toddler, had to endure the lengthy car rides, the thick pool air, the echoing ring of coaches shouting, starter guns going off, and the narrow sitting area. By the time she was four or five, she began vomiting in the car every time they took the trip, overcome by motion sickness on the forty-five-minute ride over the New Jersey highways. "I used Mr. Clean to clean it up," says Lillian. "Wherever I went I smelled like vomit. We were doing this because Lynn had to go swimming. There was no choice. At least we did not think there was any. We just did it."

In 1968, the year Martin Luther King Jr. and Senator Bobby Kennedy were assassinated, the year Lyndon Johnson decided not to seek reelection, the year Vietnam protesters began really making the news, Lynn set a record in the 100-meter breaststroke on her way to a win at the Eastern Championships. While all these tremendous national changes swirled around them, Lynn and her father were in their own little bubble, sweating it out around the long, aqua rectangle that had begun to control their lives. Swimming had become Lynn's full-time job, and her family began focusing all of its resources and aspirations on her success.

Rutgers University was too far away for the extra morning workouts that are the trademark of most serious swimmers, so Frank began taking his daughter to the YMCA in Perth Amboy, an old-fashioned sports center where down-and-out single men lived in rooms on the upper floor. In the dark of the predawn, before anyone was awake on their modest street, Lynn and her dad would trek to the car and drive twenty minutes to the Y. Even in the summer, the air over the indoor pool seemed shockingly cool. Upon first contact with the water, all the sleep would leave Lynn's young body. It took several laps before she felt the last of the chills slip away.[5]

I could dog it during team practice, because I was counting my own laps. But with my dad doing the timing and counting in the morning sessions, I did not get away with anything. I'd go all-out, while he'd time me in the 100 and 200 breaststroke. Then when I was finished, he'd say, 'Do it again, faster.' I'd feel as if my lungs were about to burst, but I'd do it again and I *would* go faster.[6]

"I remember hating it and hating my father when he felt I was not working hard enough. It was a lonely thing," Lynn said. "Then I'd go to school with my hair all wet. I do not think any athlete wants to crawl out of bed and go get wet. It was incredibly bizarre for a girl back then, what I was doing."

Because of her large size, athletic ability, and intense interest, Lynn's parents never really defined her by her girlhood. They took a more neutral approach to her life and saw her in more generic terms as a child with a talent. "There were times," Frank concedes, "when I would look at her and think, 'Boy, that's my son.'" Neighbors may have felt it all made some sense if Lynn had been a "Larry," but to be so focused on a girl's prowess seemed almost farcical. After all, Woodbridge had no local girls' swim team, and despite her string of wins, the town's newspaper rarely ran more than a paragraph on her victories. Where did the Geneskos think it would all bring them anyway?

Certainly, there were a handful of success stories in women's sports. Champions, such as Olympic sprinter Wilma Rudolph and tennis star Billie Jean King, had wheedled their way into the national consciousness with their exploits. But their fame did little to make girls' sports popular at the local level. In the end, the thrill of pleasing her father and the joy of winning drove Lynn. When she won the Eastern Championship, "It was unforgettable. I got out of the pool in an absolute daze. I did not believe I had won. My teammates were crowding around, and there were lots of other people too, and they were all congratulating me. I was so confused that I thought I was in the locker room and started taking off my bathing suit. It was down to my waist before I realized where I was. Unforgettable."

The pressure to continue her string of successes began to build within herself and within her family. Her father set up a bench in the basement that had a pulley and weight system. He figured that an extra hour a day on the weight machine would really improve the strength in Lynn's shoulders and arms. He called them "dry land" workouts. Today, when Frank talks about her training methods, Lynn shakes her head and mouths the words "sick, sick." But when she was a young girl, she did not know anything else and felt driven by her father and something inside herself to keep training. After the Eastern Championships, she accepted her swimming as a full-time job. "Not a fun one," she adds. "It was not about having a good time anymore." It was about success and winning or placing in more than 180 races.[7] The family never had time to take summer holidays. All their spare hours away from work and school went toward Lynn's swimming career.

Her life as a girl athlete isolated her from her peers. The other kids in her junior high and high school classes often spent their evenings hanging out at the Reo Diner on Amboy Avenue, chugging shakes and playing mindless tricks on the waitresses. Lynn would spend her evenings swimming laps at Rutgers University then come home, work on the pulley bench, do some homework, and then go to bed. Before the sun rose, she would be up and out at least three mornings a week to the Perth Amboy Y, her dad following with a stopwatch around his neck.[8]

Even when she became state champion in the breaststroke, even when she went to the nationals, few locals paid her successes much mind. People just did not follow girls' sports. Until high school, Lynn seemed to get enough positive feedback from her parents' obvious pride in her accomplishments and her own wall of ribbons and trophies. But when she won first place in the National Championships in Ohio in 1971 and came home to the silence, she began to resent it. "The football team was not even county champs, but they got the pep rallies and the press and the this and the that and I was like, 'Gee.' You know? Compared to the athleticism I showed, they had none of the skills I had and none of the success level. Unless I went around telling people no one knew, and I was not the kind of person to go around telling people."

In the face of such indifference from the community, Lynn pressed on. As the Olympic trials approached, she did not have time for fun; she did not have time for pitching in on Saturdays to help clean the house. She just trained, did her homework, and trained some more. Her parents expected nothing more on the home front and nothing less in the pool.

The dramatic switch that has become the trademark of contemporary girlhood today had already happened in the Genesko family: their eldest daughter's achievements outside the home took precedence over any responsibilities she might have inside the home. Nothing, not even her parents' jobs or a second child, was allowed to come between Lynn and her sports goals. And so little Caroline got sent to a sitter and had to endure the draining rides to Rutgers. For years both parents snuck out of work, taking unapproved time off, so they could get their daughter to swim practice.

But as the Olympic trials neared, Lynn pulled a muscle in her chest and had to cut back on her training. A head cold lingered. Her times dropped. By the cut-off date, she had failed to swim a qualifying time. Last year's National Champion in the 100-meter breaststroke did not make the U.S. team. Something unraveled in Lynn. The piece of herself that had kept her in it, kept her around despite the cold mornings, the wet hair, the endless laps, the relentless dad, broke. She vowed never to swim again and hung up her suit. "No one could talk to me for a month. I began running a few miles a day to get the whole thing out of my system."

Even today, when the family talks about this enormous turning point in Lynn's athletic life, tension lingers. "I had to jump all over her and convince her," Frank says, shaking with emotion. "Convince me of what, Dad?" Lynn asks. "That you were on duty and do not quit." He leaves the room. "Why is that a sad thing?" Lynn asks softly.[9]

Freed from the rigors of her training schedule, Lynn had the time and energy to explore other things. She took charge of her high school literary magazine, "El Dorado," and started joining in on the late-night runs to the Reo Diner. An enormous shopping mall went up near her house, which gave kids like her a chance to earn some money. She smoked some pot and let her hair grow long and heavy. But her swimming past would not go away.

As she closed in on her senior year, her parents decided to contact an agent about getting her a college sports scholarship. Lillian had never gone to college and vowed that things would be different for her daughters. Frank felt all those years of training would just be a waste if Lynn did not use them to at least get herself into a good university. What neither parent realize was that no girl had ever received an athletic scholarship to a major college program in the United States.[10] They kept seeing their daughter as this neutral person, a child with a talent, but society continued to see her as a girl. Her high school did nothing to market her talents. And when she hung up her suit, there were just a few whispers of regret from the local community. But Frank Genesco persisted and tracked down Bill Serra, a sports agent who often matched top male athletes with Division I college programs. Serra told Frank and Lillian that they had nothing to lose; they only had to pay if he was successful.[11]

The year Lynn failed to make the Olympic team, Congress passed Title IX. Some elite teams realized early that the future of women's sports looked a lot like the men's. If they wanted to be in the lead, they would have to start building their big-time girls' programs the same way they built their boys'. So when Bill Serra started marketing a nationally ranked female swimmer with good grades, Title IX had created an audience for him that had never existed before.[12] The University of Tennessee and American University offered acceptances, but no cash. Only the University of Miami in Florida, which had a top-ten men's swim program and wanted to build up a comparable women's program, came up with a full scholarship. For the first time in the history of big-time college sports, women athletes were being offered money. The University of Miami eventually handed out fifteen scholarships to women that year, Lynn Genesko's being one of them.[13]

Lynn does not remember having a choice. She does not remember the University of Tennessee or American University saying, "Please come!" Her father dealt with all the recruiters, the letters, and the agent. Just the trip to the University of Miami stays in her mind. They treated her like a somebody. She walked the campus, went out to dinner, and saw the beaches. "I thought, a college near the beach! I think I'll go here."[14]

For the first time, her high school and her community could not ignore her achievements. CBS came to town and trailed Lynn for a day. "The TV people came here and followed me around so that was sort of a big deal. Very exciting!" Girls had finally arrived in big-time college sports and Woodbridge, New Jersey, had produced one of its stars. Bill Serra got his $1,000 fee, and the Geneskos' daughter had a free ride to college.[15]

In that sweet summer after receiving the acceptance and money from the University of Miami, Lynn must have felt a lightness that she never expected to feel again after she missed the cut for the Olympic trials. After all the laps, all the drills, and all the summers spent skipping vacations so the family could go to her meets, Lynn's swimming had produced something tangible. But when she looks back on that time, she cannot even remember if she saw herself on television after CBS left town and aired its story. After a year away from the pool, a sense of distance had developed between Lynn and the aqua rectangle that had controlled her childhood. She went with the momentum. She went to Miami, but inside she could sense that she was on the wrong ride.[16]

She returned to the pool in Florida, but without the fierceness she had had in her early teens. "I tried to show up relatively regularly, but I did not fit in. I wanted to listen to the Grateful Dead. It was 1973 man." She dropped out after her first year "in shame. My parents thought I was out of my mind. Here I had a four-year scholarship and I left."

As a middle-class girl growing up on a typical street in Woodbridge, New Jersey, Lynn Genesko's childhood reflected both the good and the bad that has come from moving girls goals and duties outside the home. For a time, her great success with swimming boosted her self-confidence and kept her focused on productive things, such as good grades. The self-discipline required to endure the grueling workouts became a lifelong habit that she tapped into as an adult to great effect.

But years of dragging Caroline to swim meets soured the relationship between the sisters. It created a divide that has not healed and probably would not have existed if Lynn had lived in a time in which taking care of her baby sister was an important part of her day-to-day chores. The fact that she and her parents went to such extreme lengths with her sports interest, and made swimming a kind of job, meant both the positive and negative effects were extreme as well.

When she looks back on her childhood, Lynn knows her parents just tried to give her what they thought she wanted. But somewhere along the line they all made the crucial decision to make Lynn's outside interest more important than nearly anything else. The Geneskos' sports-obsessed life marked the beginning of a massive trend in American culture: family lives centered around children's sports events, rather than the household economy or familial obligations, such as visiting with relatives on the weekend. The more swimming became the primary duty of Lynn's life, the more dependent she became on that sole strand for her stability. To regain her equilibrium, she recognized that she had to leave her "job," even if it meant giving up her historic scholarship. She turned her back on the Florida coast and headed home to start over.[17]

2000. At first I thought I wanted to profile a family that reflected many of the problems I highlight in this book, but then I realized that it was painfully easy to find a sample subject. It seems everywhere I look I see girls who were into sports when they were ten years old suddenly become confused and uninvolved now that they are in high school. True to Joan Brumberg's observations in The Body Project, so many young daughters today obsess about their clothes and do little of consequence for their families on a day-to-day basis. As the mother of a nine-year-old girl, I stress over my own role as tool giver to my child. What am I doing to make sure that when she hits her teen years she will feel competent, useful, and loved? As a former college athlete, I am tempted to think her experiences in sports will give her what she needs, but I see every day how untrue and hollow this backup plan has become. The building must begin on the home front; but how?

So I started my quest for a family that worked well in the face of all the pressures of modern society. I contacted friends from various school districts around the country who asked teachers, principals, and counselors to identify families with confident girls. From one town I received several notes with the same family name on them: Hodgkins. They had three daughters ages ten to eighteen, whom everyone agreed excelled in school, sports, and, more important, in general self-esteem. While the Hodgkins live a comfortable middle-class life, they are not affluent and attend public schools in a system in which their white skin makes them a minority. The eldest is a senior at the local high school, which has more than twenty-five hundred students. To nearly everyone who has come in contact with them, they represent a slice of mainstream America that is working and I set off to find out why.[1]

MEGGY, ALLY, AND SARAH
"We were good enough; we could do it"

The smells in the training room were not middle school smells. They belonged to something much stronger: to young men in from the football field. When Ally Hodgkins, an eighth grader, had seen high school girls taping ankles on the sidelines of her older sister's soccer games, "it seemed like fun." Most of the year Ally played soccer as well, or basketball, but every fall only the demands of homework structured her after-school hours. "It got so boring, so I talked to my dad about being a trainer for the high school, and he thought it would be good. I'd meet other kids and learn about injuries."

But watching a few girls work on ankles in an open field did not prepare Ally for the sense of smallness that would overcome her when she entered the bustling trainer's room. Half-dressed players milled between the tables, many of them twice the size of her dad. Their voices thrummed the air, which was heavy with sweat and the sweet medicine smell of body rub.

The head trainer told Ally that "they'd never had an eighth grader work out before. They always got discouraged. So that got me scared. All the other trainers were eleventh graders and one was a senior. The first day my sister [Sarah] sat with me and the second day and the third. She just sat there." Ally flicks her long brown ponytail playfully as she says this and shines a smile that reveals braces. "I did not know anyone there. I'd sit in the car before I'd go into the high school and tell my mother I did not like it. She said I had to just do it for two weeks and then we could talk about it."

"She was having a miserable experience," quips Sarah, a senior at the high school.

After about a week, Ally did not need her big sister around anymore. She had learned some of the basic taping techniques and made some casual friends. For away games she sat in the front seat of the bus, while behind her rows of teenage football players got hyped for the game. The energy level, the attention, the intensity were unlike anything she had seen as a girl playing sports in the city.

The head trainers gave her a checklist of skills she had to master. They showed her how to wrap a figure eight around an ankle so the tape would not bunch, but still would hit the joint that needed the most support. "I had to learn and practice for awhile. If I got it right, they'd check it off." She progressed to wrists, elbows, and knees. The greater her skill with the tape, the more open and confident she became with everyone around her, including the male athletes she worked with. "One day my dad picked me up and I had to tell him I'd had a good day in the training room," Ally says with a laugh.

The Hodgkins family lives in a simple brick house in a city of 120,000 people outside of a much larger city that could be anywhere in the United States: Los Angeles, Boston, Cleveland, Chicago. The seasons change where they are, so the mature maple in their front yard flushes yellow every autumn and drops leaves that glitter like gold pieces. The three daughters—Meggy, age ten; Ally, age thirteen; and Sarah, age eighteen—attend public schools where blacks and Hispanics outnumber whites. The Hodgkins are white.

The parents—Cindy and Ken—grew up in Maine, a world away from the urban life their daughters live. With Ken working full time and Cindy working part time, they have managed to accrue the basics of middle-class life: their own home, two cars, a new puppy. One thing they also have, which many American families want but cannot seem to "build," are three confident daughters

Like most middle-class modern daughters, the Hodgkins girls have few responsibilities at home. They have to clean their own rooms, though Meggy often gets help from her older sister Sarah, who has to do extra chores to help pay off her growing telephone bill. (Her boyfriend attends a college out of state.) For a time, Ally and Sarah alternated nights for dish duty, but they started leaving the worst pans to soak until the next day, which led to feuding. Mom's solution: She now makes them do the dishes together every night. "The less they get along, the more I have them do together," Cindy says as her wide smile lifts her glasses a notch on her nose. "In the end, doing the dishes together has been a lot more fun," says Ally. "We talk a lot."

They just added a dog to the family mix, after years of pleading from the kids, which particularly excited Meggy, who was tired of "being the youngest in the family." All three of them help take care of the new "baby," an overly friendly, overweight, tongue-wagging black lab.

Mary Ellen Todd, who crossed the United States with her family on their move to Oregon in 1852, would have found the Hodgkins girls' list of physical chores—dishes, bedrooms, dog—unbelievably light, even frivolous. There is no greasing of the wagon wheels or taking care of a deathly ill parent in this brick split-level house. Yet Meggy, Ally, and Sarah display the same kind of competence and confidence that sings forth from Mary Ellen's stories. Obviously, the answer to the Hodgkins' success lies outside the traditional duties assigned to daughters during the nineteenth century. Somehow their parents have guided them and they have guided themselves to a balanced sense of self-worth, even as the modern world spins around them at a pace Mary Ellen—used to the measured step of the oxen—would have found unthinkable.

One answer: soccer games. Lots of them. When he had three daughters, Ken knew he would have to take some deliberate steps if he hoped to sustain a close relationship with them. A trim, intense man with brown eyes and closely cut brown hair, he grew up loving skiing and sports in general. "After the third one was born, he felt for him to spend time with them they would need a common thread, so he was the one who pushed soccer," says Cindy. "He felt too many girls work as individuals and do not work for one common goal."

"In high school, I got my best grades when doing a sport," Ken says, then grows silent while fingering the back of a chair. Cindy jumps in talking, with the two older girls interrupting from time to time. Soccer clearly makes them feel animated.

To keep it a family experience rather than something that divided them between fields and game times, Ken coached their teams. The league made sure the games were on the same field and were played back to back. "We did spend Sunday in the car," says Cindy, with her Maine twang and forthright stare, "but we spent it together in the car."

Sarah led the way for the others. "As a typical first girl, I did not like contact when I was young. I'd be doing my hair during a game. To tell you the truth, I hated it at first. My parents told me to stick in there. Then I tried out for some select team and found I was not as bad as I thought."

Once the coed league split into single-sex teams in the second grade, Sarah no longer had the role of youngest girl on a mixed team. "All of a sudden I just loved it. I started to make good friends. I became more outgoing. I became one of the stronger players on the team—there's a hierarchy there—and I was no longer the quiet young girl anymore. Besides all the girls on the team loved my dad. They thought he was really cool. I can't remember a single event or meet that there was not a member of my family there," says Sarah, who looks remarkably like Cindy when she smiles. "One time my mom drove back to the beach after visiting with some friends just so she could be there for the second half of my game. It was something really important to them. So many kids I play with, their moms cannot come because they want to finish watching their soap opera or something."

The two younger girls saw Sarah's joy in soccer and joined teams as well. Meggy's league for girls under eleven still meets just twice a week, but Ally and Sarah have reached the age at which practices and games fill their lives. The two older girls branched out into track, basketball, and training room work as well, so sports dominate their schedule throughout the school year. They feel it builds up their confidence and keeps them busy in positive ways. "At school they used to let the boys play basketball and the girls just sort of hung around. But a group of my friends who played [basketball] with me, asked if we could play," Ally says, still flipping her ponytail. "We were good enough. We could do it. So we started playing with them."

Meggy, a slender girl with straight blond hair, blue eyes, and freckles, remains far more reserved than her dark-haired, dark-eyed athletic sisters, whose words tumble over each other when in conversation. As the youngest, she enjoys soccer but is just as happy to spend an afternoon with her new dog. Even with television, movies, and mass marketing pressing in on her young psyche, Meggy has managed to remain true to age ten and all the imaginary worlds that can entail. When asked about some of her favorite things, she immediately mentions *Gladis*, the faded wreck of a ship that sits on the lawn of the house where her mother grew up in Maine. The Hodgkins family retreats to the coolness of northern New England every summer for at least eight weeks. By the beach, in the sun, Meggy, and her many young cousins who live there year-round, "sail" *Gladis* or spend hours making rooms full of furniture out of the stones along the shoreline. Tables, chairs, a walkway. "It's fantasy world," says Cindy with a light laugh, cherishing the thought that she still has one young enough to play such games.

The trips to Maine, which the flexibility of Cindy's part-time job make possible, prove a vital breaking-off point from the intense, highly scheduled life the family lives in the city. Unlike many other families with sports-obsessed kids, the Hodgkins walk away from it all—the summer camps, the summer league play—for the sake of something much more important to them: family time. They leave a week after school ends and do not return until the week before school begins. At first Sarah, the eldest, thought she would miss out on too much if she left town for so long, but "after a year or two of worrying about that I realized that when I came back I had not missed anything. Most of my friends were just hanging out." Ally, on the other hand, has always loved going. "I like the freedom. In Maine I can walk around with my friends because it's secluded there. There's a lot to do here, but there's more to do over the summer there that I found interesting. There's five or six kids my age on the island. Even if we did not do anything, it's just fun to be around them all day. We'll go swimming or fishing. Sometimes we go on the boat. Our families have a Boston Whaler."

Their uncle had a lobster boat for a time. Sarah once worked as a sternman for him as a summer job. "My uncle would pull up the trap. I'd open it up and he'd measure to see if they were long enough. While he was doing that, I'd take the old bait off and stick a nasty fish head on the hooks. Then I'd band the claws. It smelled pretty bad. But it sure beat working at McDonald's. I'd be out there all day. I could wear my bathing suit. Listen to music."

Meggy has gone out on her uncle's boat as well, although he switched to crabbing a few years back. "Whenever they go out they catch all these crabs. There's two big holes in the hold. If you look down, it's just full of crabs," Meggy said.

When the girls speak of Maine, it is as though a piece of the place enters the living room where they sit. Their experiences there have left them with something tangible that they can finger when the urban life around them presses in too hard. Sarah's years in Maine taught her not to take life in the city too seriously. "It taught me how insignificant" it can all be—even the soccer, which she cares enough about to be good at, but not so much that it controls her life. When applying for colleges, she purposely looked at excellent schools with solid soccer programs rather than big-time soccer programs with a mediocre academic reputation. "Soccer would be her whole life at those schools and she does not want that," says Cindy. But Sarah has thought about applying to a good school close to home so she can make it to some of her sisters' soccer games. Cindy adds, "Family is such an important part of her upbringing that she hates not being part of their lives."

Cindy uses connectedness as a measuring stick in every aspect of their day-to-day life. When the girls began feuding over what shows they wanted to watch, she made television completely off-limits during the school week. "When Ally started school, I wanted to eliminate things that would create stress. If a half an hour a day this person is watching this show and another a different show, it divides them. I do not want them off watching different shows."

Ally smiles when Sarah remarks that the no-TV rule hit the middle sister hardest. "I got used to it," Ally counters. "I do not care anymore." They have clearly reached a cheery agreement, but Cindy acknowledges it was hard at first. "But I'm a very strong-willed person," she says, then pauses, "and so are my girls." She laughs.

The computer has proven less of a battle over use and more of a proving ground for building trust. All of the girls use the computer to sustain their contacts with their cousins in Maine, so Cindy sees that as something that builds family ties. Both she and Ken have spoken bluntly with the girls about where they can and cannot go on the Internet. To them it is no different then telling them what neighborhoods to avoid. "I never go into a public chat room or anything," says Ally, the heaviest computer user. She often gives her parents tips on how to use the Internet more effectively and spends hours each week "instant messaging" her cousins.

For all their savvy with modern technology, the girls look remarkably untouched by their time. Unlike the mass of suburban kids who wear clothes that trumpet names such as Tommy Hiflinger, the Hodgkins' wardrobe is decidedly neutral. The girls wear basic cotton tops with stripes or solid colors, and simple pants or sweats. The only jewelry Sarah, who goes to college next fall, wears is a silver watch. "She actually bought a little bit of eye shadow and lip gloss to go to homecoming last weekend. It was the first makeup she'd ever purchased." Cindy confides. "I asked her about that and you know what her comment was: The less-confident girls wear more makeup. If you're happy with how you look, you do not use it. I will never forget the day Sarah came home and all she wanted to wear was Umbro shorts and T-shirts. I was really upset because it's the whole brand-name thing. Ken looked at me and said, 'We have a twelve-year-old daughter and all she wants to wear is Umbro shorts and a T-shirt and we're going to complain!' Girls can be tough on each other," Cindy concedes, "but my three remain relatively low key and easygoing with clothes."

In the past a drought might have brought a family together, or a lost job, or simply the labor required for day-to-day chores in the days before electricity. In the current time of plenty and advancing technology, parents must choose their rallying points more deliberately. Both Cindy and Ken recognized this from the start and made countless deliberate decisions that reinforced the family's commitment to each other. Cindy, in particular, as the primary caretaker, has made it clear to the girls that they have no higher responsibility than to be there for one another. If they feud over the television, the television is shut off. If they fight over dishes, they have to do them together. If they all want to play soccer, they do it on the same day in the same place and cheer each other on. If they want to go shopping, mom comes along. No daughter hops off to the mall with a credit card in hand and no supervision.

Even in the unstructured haven of Maine, connectedness rules. In July the girls can invite friends up to stay at the family's large homestead, but in August they move to a much smaller cabin where they spend the final August days just with each other. "I've seen so many times when kids are not really with their parents," Cindy says. "They invite other kids over to play all weekend. We never did a lot of that. We did things as a family. Maine is an important part of raising my girls," Cindy claims, but she does not think people need a house in Maine to do what she's doing. "I've tried as hard as I can to give them as many tools as I can. The problem with our day and age is we do not give them the tools. We sign them up for kindergarten as early as we can or we use sports as a baby-sitter. Many parents spend a lot of time working and a lot of time with their kids when they're not really with their kids. I made a lot of decisions to be available. I do work but have still found a way to be there. The first fifteen minutes after they come in that door I hear 90 percent of the information I'm going to hear for the day. I know exactly what's happening with who their friends are and their teachers."

It is clear Cindy expects her girls to be "available" to each other as well, which is why Sarah sat in the trainer room with Ally for several days in a row. Having her mom there would have horrified Ally, who already felt starkly young in the high school setting. At least her sister went to the school and knew many of the athletes and trainers.

As they mature it will no longer be the youngest needing the oldest but all of them linked to each other in a web Cindy and Ken hope will help them ward off whatever blows come their way. "Friends come and go," muses Sarah. "But my sisters I'll have forever. I'll spend Christmas with them for the next twenty years!"

Earlier, when Sam lamented the loss of her uncle's lobstering business, she had joked a bit about doing it herself, fish heads and all. She and Ally laughed as they sat on the couch, then looked at each other with the splendid kind of connectedness Cindy has worked so hard to forge between them. "Heck," Sarah says, "Ally could do it with me!"

CONCLUSION
A Domestic Revival

The fact that many of the girls in this book canned vegetables, washed clothes by hand, embroidered lace, sewed their own clothes, baby-sat siblings, planted gardens, pulled weeds, and stoked fires all by the time they were the age of ten, does not really provide any answers for today's society. Americans simply do not live such a labor-intensive life anymore. So what lesson can modern parents steal from the past? Families who taught their children skills they deemed necessary for the well-being of the household raised children who gained a sense of self-worth that endured. Neither peers, personal loss, nor cultural trends could shake it loose.

As a strong advocate for equal rights for girls at every level, I did not want to accept the fact that some daughters in the past, who had been denied a decent education and any chance of a career, actually grew up to become more centered adults than most of the teenagers I know today. Was having a vital role in the household really that crucial to self-respect? After years of research I have concluded that it is.

The time is ripe for a domestic revival in the United States. The horrible attacks on the World Trade Center in New York City on September 11, 2001, and subsequent terrorist activity, underscore the need for a stronger home base for children today. As the larger world around them becomes increasingly chaotic, their role at home could serve as succor. When Connie Sullivan's world seemed to fall apart during the Depression, she took strength from the fact that she could contribute to her family in its time of need. Small gestures such as doing the dishes, cooking dinner, or pitching in 78 cents actually made her feel less afraid.

DIVVYING UP HOUSEHOLD WORK

Few American children today have an opportunity to play such a fulfilling role in their households. Recent sociological studies show that if the mother works full time, the average daughter does about ten hours of housework a week.[1] This seems like a substantial contribution, and it is, but not one that anyone else in the household values or aspires to. The sons in these same households get away with doing three hours or less of chores a week (370). The unspoken assumption remains remarkably old fashioned: They have more important things to train for than taking care of a household. Of course now girls may think they have more important things to do too, but since they may be saddled with the dual obligation of sustaining a career and a home life, they still take it more seriously than their brothers.

Because domestic work has become so devalued in general, even daughters will skip out on household obligations at the first opportunity. If a mother works part time, all of the children beg off the chores and do less than two hours of chores a week.[2] And while dads are stepping up more around the house in the last decade, most of the extra work they take on are chores that children normally do, not mothers, so they rarely lighten their wives' loads and just further distance the children from the domestic cycle.[3] In short, dad and the children do less than one-quarter of the chores in even the most egalitarian of households.[4] Daughters do more than sons if pushed, but certainly not with pride.

To return sons and daughters to a more legitimate and fulfilling role at home, Americans must first break down negative and sexist attitudes about housework as well as social habits that encourage isolation and self-serving behavior. The average child age eight to eighteen spends nearly seven hours a day with some form of media. At least half of the children of those ages have a television in their bedroom and 60 percent sit down to dinner with the boob tube blaring.[5]

When Cindy Hodgkins noticed her three daughters retreating to their separate bedrooms to watch three different television shows, she realized that television had become a dividing force in her family. She set up new rules that kept the television off during the school week. On the weekends they have one central set in the living room that the children can watch together for a few hours.

When the three sisters squirreled away in their bedrooms, they did not deal with each other and they did not learn any skill that anyone would value in the long run. On the Oregon Trail, Mary Ellen's stepmother taught the children how to start a fire with buffalo chips and make breakfast for six or more people. How many parents today even expect their nine year olds to rinse their own cereal bowl? How many families even bother to eat breakfast together (with the television off) before the kids head to school? Fewer and fewer.

The fact that many of the shows children watch foster damaging stereotypes about domestic work means that too much media exposure not only isolates people but also encourages sexist behavior. Studies show that sitcoms, in particular, present household work as drudgery best left to girls, and children who watch these shows are far more apt to embrace these attitudes.[6]

On a subtle level, all of the sports programs that Americans engage in with such fervor and pride actually divide families. Schools used to sponsor teams. Children went straight from their last class to the playing fields then home in time for dinner. Games were held during the week, which left the weekends free for family functions. Youngsters in grammar school did not compete in any organized sports; they just played pick-up games of kickball or tag in their neighborhoods. Today, a six-year-old might miss his dinner or a relative's graduation for the sake of a soccer game. Twelve-year-olds get on travel teams that often have to stay overnight on weekends for away games. The entire process reflects a complete disregard for a child's need, and right, to spend a substantial amount of time with his or her family. The children begin to lose perspective and become irate with parents who do not take their sports "career" as seriously as they do. Family time may be on the rise, as recent sociological studies have claimed, but much of that time boils down to shuttling kids around from one game to another.[7] The athletes have no time to play a substantial role on the home front.

What did the Genesko family gain by giving up their summer vacations for all those years so Lynn could travel to swim meets? The Hodgkins girls, who drop soccer every July and August so they can be with their family in Maine, have found a way to reap splendid benefits from sports without sacrificing their family commitments. Like the Sullivans, they learned that nothing they do in their outside life should come at the expense of their domestic life.

Few American mothers have found the balance that Cindy Hodgkins has achieved. Overwhelmed and underappreciated, many of these women have turned outward for hired help. They see domestic work as something that must be dealt with like an intrusion, not as the unifying thread it once was in the past. Thanks to an incredibly cheap immigrant labor pool, people from all sorts of economic backgrounds can afford to hire gardeners, maids, nannies, cooks, and drivers. A Pizza Hut manager, a plumber, and a cashier are just a few of the clients on the list at Maria Anderson, a service agency in southern California.[8] Farming out domestic work has become an acceptable part of life for many Americans.

When children watch other people handle the lawn, the laundry, even the cooking, they learn very little about how to participate in their own domestic life. They know to stay out of the way and, perhaps, to pick up their clothes when the maid comes to vacuum, but they are becoming increasingly disconnected from the household economy they rely on for food, clean clothes, and shelter and the work required to sustain it.

When Benjamin Franklin penned his essay, "For Those Who Would Remove to America" in 1784, he spent most of his time bragging about the domestic skills of American men and women, who tilled their own fields, made their own bread, and sewed their own clothes. "Very few are rich enough to live idly upon their rents or incomes," he wrote, with pride. A "happy mediocrity prevails," he claimed,[9] precisely because the family-based economy meant few became immensely rich or desperately poor.

Henry David Thoreau saw a very different America just sixty years later when he wrote *Walden*. He chastised his neighbors for spending all their time working so they could buy more things. Even the farmers, he felt, toiled all day so they could beget more "comforts," and seemed quite willing to let other people build and make all the substantive things in their lives, such as their clothes. "Where is all this division of labor to end?" he exclaimed. "Before we can adorn our houses with beautiful objects the walls must be stripped and our lives must be stripped, and beautiful housekeeping and beautiful living be laid for a foundation."[10] When Thoreau wrote of beautiful housekeeping, he certainly was not thinking of Martha Stewart's billion-dollar home-decorating empire.

The terrible deterioration in domestic skills and social ties has continued apace since the mid-nineteenth century and made home an especially chaotic place for people who have no skilled immigrants to hire or competent family members to turn to. The tidy well-ordered worlds of the office and the mall have become havens for overstretched parents and restless children. Many find it easier to carve out personal space in these more public spaces than at home, a trend that further erodes a family's ability to be together. The thirteen-year-old daughter goes to the mall to see her friends and shop for fun rather than clean her room. Mother and father are off shuffling another sibling to an away game, so there is no one around to ensure that she does this basic chore. In the end, the two children get to center their days on their needs and nothing gets accomplished on the home front.

In today's urban, high-tech society, there is no going back to a frontierlike existence, so much of which was tedious anyway. And no one with any compassion could ask women to return to the confining expectations for homemakers common in the 1950s, just so everyone else can have a fuller home life. But society has to do something to recover its domestic spirit or America's sons and daughters risk growing up with nothing more to center themselves on than sports games, mass media, and shopping. As Lynn Genesko's failed Olympic quest showed, that is a shaky foundation at best, and intensely damaging to family relations at worst.

SOLUTIONS IN UNEXPECTED PLACES

Some of the best models for a more involved and balanced household dynamic come from the most unexpected places. Studies show that gay couples, single parents, and black couples do a much better job, in general, of carving out household responsibilities for children and dividing those chores up evenly between the sexes.[11] A working mother with three children has to eke out all she can from everyone under her roof. Gay couples are not as caught up in sex-based roles. Studies show that many black families remain generations closer to their rural roots than their white counterparts, and the general dynamics of the more labor-intensive farm life can still be seen in their city homes. They are more apt to expect everyone to contribute and to expend energy teaching basic skills, such as mastering a family recipe.[12]

Gay couples and single-parent households are not family prototypes most Americans feel comfortable aspiring to, which is understandable given the many problems common to these two family groups, especially mothers on their own. The more important point is that gays and single parents have begun to work outside the box that has proven so damaging; more conventional two-parent couples need to learn to do the same if the institution of marriage and family will survive. One great example of some of the gains that can be made is sons of single mothers do as much work around the house as daughters from two-parent families (ibid.).

The 2000 Census showed that people living alone constituted the fastest growing type of household in America. As sociologists Frances Goldscheider and Linda Waite conclude in their book *New Families, No Families,* if we do not carve out a more equitable, fulfilling domestic cycle, today's children, especially girls, may grow up to prefer going it alone. "One factor that is clearly moving American society toward 'no families' is the weakening of the preparation among all children for making a home, with others or alone" (168).

Elizabeth Sullivan had it right back in 1937 when her son Richard announced he would no longer do the dishes because it was "girl's work." Every time he went to use a spoon, plate, or cup, she grabbed it out of his hand. If he would not wash it, he could not use it. His resolve faded as his hunger grew. He gave in by dinner that day. With the same kind of tenacity, Americans must push their sons and husbands toward a more equitable role in the household cycle.

Since 1980 millions more people have worked at home, a trend that opens up great possibilities for rejuvenating domestic life. Families could return to the more natural patterns of the farmers and artisans who worked in small cottage industries before the Industrial Revolution. Back then the men were apt to do outdoor chores, such as handling livestock, while the women stayed inside to cook, clean, and care for the children. In today's society, in which few fathers are handling pigs in the barnyard, American's need a new mind-set to apply to their old-fashioned home-based workforce. Men and boys are just as apt as females in the house to be pushing paper or scrolling text on a screen. The vital challenge in the new domestic cycle is whether families can divide chores up evenly and without bias and whether they can make their children feel that their contributions are valued, even essential.

American society has grown too complex to expect simply skills, such as bread making, to revitalize peoples' home lives. One-half of all children eventually live with a divorced parent. Nearly one-third of American families are headed by a single mother, which helps explain why so many women with young children have jobs outside the home. Many of these people work away from their households all day and return exhausted to their kitchens and their children sometime after 6 P.M.

Public organizations, such as schools, need to get more involved. To really see how far Americans have distanced themselves from building household economies, think of what coaches and students would say if public high schools required all students in after-school programs to break from their activities one afternoon a week so they could cook dinner for their families. Volunteers and teachers could collect money, purchase ingredients, and oversee the cooking in the onsite home economics kitchens. No one, not even the vaunted football players, would be exempt. Working parents, single parents, even at-home mothers could look forward to a midweek break from pulling together supper for the family. That's a much more useful thing to bring home than another sweaty T-shirt, more stories about problems with the coach, or bullies in the after-school care program. The same people who claim that the logistics for such an enterprise would be too daunting spend hours and hours each week ferrying their children to soccer games, lining up intricate "travel team" schedules, and more. The issue is resolve not practicality.

I attended a high school that required all students to take on a janitorial job, such as mopping the cafeteria floors or collecting trash in the enormous school garbage truck. No one was exempt. The end result: The school saved hundreds of thousands of dollars on salaries normally paid to support staff and taught each child that mundane tasks can be an important way to build community.

REEDUCATING PARENTS

One reason why the domestic cycle has become an irrelevant sideshow in most American homes is that the parents have so few skills to pass on to their children. Overworked and poorly skilled mothers and fathers often throw money at the problem. If you do not know how to cook the holiday turkey, why not "spend $128, plus tax," for the Martha Stewart turkey cooking kit, jokes author Elizabeth Austin in a *Washington Monthly* article. "You get an instruction booklet, a 6-inch trussing needle, a spool of cotton twine, a stainless steel roasting pan and adjustable rack, a baster, a thermometer, a pastry brush, a fat separator and cheesecloth."[13] Of course Martha is betting that the average American no longer has most of these items in their kitchen, and she is right.

Austin admits she can "whip up a bittersweet chocolate-and-mandarin orange cheesecake good enough to rub in your hair. I can do exquisite white-on-white embroidery, fashioning elaborate flowers and glossy leaves from a skein of thread. Yet, I do not think I could plan, purchase, and prepare a week's worth of family meals or sew a simple dress if you held a gun to my head. When it comes to homemaking, I am an idiot savant" (A1).

Most American men and women in Austin's age bracket—late thirties—could say the same thing. One reason why our children do not feel essential at home anymore is because their parents have no idea what to tell them to do. Kaile Warren Jr. of Maine built an $8 million Hire-a-Hus-band business around one basic fact: "No one hands down carpentry skills anymore." His twenty-nine franchises are now part of a $9 billion handyman industry. The shift is no less dramatic on the "wife" side of the equation. Many studies predict that within the next five years more than half of all meals will be prepared outside the home.[14]

So adults muddle through on their own or rely on Martha Stewart, Hire-A-Husband, or some other commercial cover-up for answers. The ignorance grows with each successive generation, creating a gash in the domestic cycle that drives children outward into the arms of test scores, the media, sports teams, and other, often ruthless, forms of measurement.

REBUILDING DOMESTIC OBLIGATIONS

On every level of society Americans need to stop focusing so in-tensely on preparing children for the workplace and independent suc-cess and, instead, think about giving them the tools they will need as adults to form thriving families. As Austin argues, "No one—male or fe-male—should graduate from high school without demonstrating the ability to run a washing machine, fry an egg, balance a checkbook, compile a grocery list and use a power drill."[15]

To rebuild the home base parents will have to broaden their concept of "family" to include extended relatives, peer groups, and public or-ganizations such as schools. After-school programs can have domestic agendas for their students that make it clear that extracurricular activ-ities sometimes have to take a backseat to family commitments. In-stead of expecting nannies who pick up the children after school to clean up around the house, have them walk the children through a se-ries of chores. Let the nanny take on the role Elizabeth Sullivan played for her son Richard.

What matters is that parents rebuild a culture of domestic obliga-tions for their children. How they do it can be as varied as the shape of families in America. They can turn to gay couples for ideas on how to divvy up chores without sexual bias. They can admire single mothers who have figured out how to get their sons to step up. They can de-mand more family-friendly schedules from sports programs.

Americans owe their daughters a home life that empowers and pro-tects even the most mediocre student, the least successful athlete. A ten-year-old can flip an egg. A twelve-year-old can mow the lawn. A six-year-old can set the table. Working within the framework of a healthy, gender-neutral domestic cycle, children do not have to be better or worse than anyone else, they can simply be contributors.

But can today's parents find the skill, time, and patience it takes to teach their children how to do chores? Can they trust their sons and daughters enough to put them in charge of basic things, such as making dinner every Wednesday night? More and more mothers and fathers say no, so they do it themselves or hire outsiders. This response has the twofold result of undermining their children's confidence and forcing them into levels of self-absorption even well-to-do eighteenth- and nineteenth-century girls, such as Lizzie and Mollie, would have found appalling. They may have had slaves to churn the butter and do the laundry, but that did not free either of them from the feeling that their families—not themselves—came first, and that they still had domestic responsibilities they had to attend to.

The only sure way to pull our daughters away from all their navel gazing in our media-saturated world is to return them to a domestic cycle that makes them feel valued and needed. This time their brothers must enter with them. The new dynamic requires each family member to return home with an open mind about their role and a commitment to make it all matter again.

EPILOGUE
The Women They Became

So many factors come into play when measuring the adult that rises out of the child. Nearly all of the girls profiled in these pages matured into confident, happy women, especially those who grew up in the eighteenth and nineteenth centuries. But their success is hardly startling since the pool is skewed. The simple fact that so many of them spoke at length about their childhood experiences to relatives, or, in the case of Lucy Larcom and Harriet Jacobs, who wrote books about it, speaks of a certain boldness on their part. From an economic standpoint, they may not have been especially wealthy or well educated, but on the character side of the equation, they stood out at an early age. I could re-create part of their girlhoods precisely because they valued themselves.

Of the girls who grew up in America prior to 1900, three of them lived very conventional lives focused on raising their families, but four balked under the rules of the day, never married, and had careers. All of them pursued balanced, productive lives with a clear sense of purpose, which is the best we could hope for for any of our daughters.

Lizzie Perkins, Mary Ellen Todd, and Mollie Gregory lived the lives their parents had prepared them to live. In Lizzie's case that meant playing wife to Samuel Cabot, a wealthy, Protestant merchant in Boston, who went into business with her father. They made an immense fortune in trade, then closed shop in 1838, a year after the great financial panic, and lived off their investments.

Samuel built a splendid house on Winthrop Place for his family in 1823, giving detailed instructions for its construction: "Round each window the end of each stone to be finely dressed to a smooth surface, as to reveal the window frames without pointing. Under each lower front window, a sunken panel, also a keyed arch over each door, the splinths, belts, window-stools, front door sills, and steps to be of the best Chelmsford stone."[1]

By the time she moved into the house, Lizzie already had four sons and a daughter. Over the next fourteen years she carried six more children, three of whom died young. Like many of her contemporaries, Lizzie lost one at birth and another in infancy, but, perhaps, even more painful, she lost her eldest son, Thomas, after he had reached adulthood. He succumbed to disease in 1826 at the age of twenty-one while working in the China office of the family trading company. Pregnant with twins at the time, of which only one survived, Lizzie weathered a parent's worst nightmare twice over that year.

People today find the regularity of such losses unfathomable. Family graveyards in eighteenth-century America are filled with small headstones, many of them for babes left nameless. Parents taught their children to have a strong faith in God precisely because they saw spiritual strength as a necessary tool in their rigorous world. Lizzie probably turned to her church, her large extended family, and to their beach house in Nahant for solace. The only reference to her state of mind around this time comes from an account left by her daughter Sarah, who was not born until 1835 but recalls hearing stories from her older siblings. "She was very much run down and my brother Edward had cholera," she writes (290). At least Edward survived.

Financially, the family continued to prosper, however, and by 1851 Samuel Cabot was building yet another house for his growing brood. Sarah recalls:

The house was built while mother was abroad. Behind it was a very large square yard, backing up against another large yard with elm trees in it and an old-fashioned wooden house with a sloping roof.

Our nursery, where we spent our mornings, was at the back of the house with the sun on it all day and Nunnie always with us. I slept in bed with her— a very large and soft feather bed. In the morning she would get up and begin the day by washing the fireplace and hearth with soapsuds, before she made the fire. She had her hands full with us when we were very small. We lived out of doors, playing close to her. She lived with my mother 50 years, dying when she was 80. (298)

Through her daughter's account it is possible to piece together some of Lizzie's adult life, complete with trips to London, a beach house, lots of servants, and an enormous immediate and extended family, including her sisters, her father, her in-laws, and her cousin Jim Cushing, who had created a museum with her when they were children.

Like her mother, Lizzie essentially supervised the domestic cycle of a well-to-do family. She told others what to do and where to go. She educated her daughters the way she had been educated, at a local dame school taught by Mary Peabody who married the author Nathaniel Hawthorne. The new house on Temple Place had a theater for the children, who performed plays just as their mother had when she was a girl.

In July 1878, just eight years before Lizzie died at the age of eighty-four, an old childhood friend sent her a letter describing their old neighborhood, which had been destroyed in "The Great Fire." "But the minutest occurrences, the words and expressions of those days remain," wrote Eliza Quincy. "I do not believe that the same period ever witnessed such changes as we have—which the power of steam and electricity have chiefly caused. The world around us is entirely new, the habits, the ideas of the people, are radically altered. We may congratulate ourselves on having lived in what I fear will prove the best period of our countries [sic] happiness and prosperity."[2] There is nothing in the historical record to indicate that Lizzie Perkins felt any less positive than her friend about her own well-defined life and the era she lived in.

The other well-to-do character in this book, Mollie Gregory, also strode in predictable steps. She married into her class when she wed Dr. Llewellyn Powell. They lived near her childhood home on Washington Street in Alexandria, Virginia, and had several children. Her obituary listed a son and daughter, but other records indicate she had, and lost, two other children: William, who was taken by tuberculosis while attending medical school, and a daughter, Neville, who died at age two-and-a-half.[3]

As a girl, of course, Mollie had watched her mother grieve the loss of Mollie's only brother, Boyd. Though still very young at the time, she recalled how her stepsisters worked constantly to calm and comfort Mrs. Gregory, who took more than a year to recover from the emotional blow. There is no record of how Mollie, who went by Mary Powell as an adult, handled her own losses, but she lived in a time when such tragedies were anticipated, if not understood.

Once her surviving children matured, Mary became the town historian and published an account of life in the city from 1741 to 1863. It came out in book form in 1928, just six months before she died at the age of eighty-one. She relished the details of her own family line, which included men who had fought with George Washington and sailed with Sir Frances Drake. She also took great pride in the role Alexandria played during the Civil War. Perhaps her own oblivious state at the time made her curious as an adult about what exactly was going on around her when she was a girl. She kept the original form her father had to sign declaring his allegiance to the Union, if he wanted to stay in his home in Alexandria. In her obituary, the writer praised her for being a dutiful doctor's wife, a good mother (her son became a well-known local doctor), a published historian, and the concerned keeper of the Grave of the Unknown Hero of the Revolution in the Old Presbyterian Church graveyard (ibid.).

Mary Ellen Todd also lived a life that closely mirrored her mother's world, but that world was a long way from the fancy drawing rooms Lizzie and Mollie knew. In 1860 Mary Ellen married John Pound Applegate in Rose City, Oregon. Conflicting records make it hard to discern how many children she had with her first husband because several died in infancy and only four of the estimated eight were living when she died in 1924 at the age of eighty-one. One of her daughters, Adrietta Applegate Hixon, decided to write down her mother's account of her journey West, which she titled *On to Oregon*.

In the foreword, Adrietta recalls riding horseback with her mother "into the Warren's mining district of Central Idaho."[4] The children also hit the trail with their parents when John Applegate drove his cattle "from his Oregon ranch to the Southern plains of Idaho, to graze them on the high bunch grass then growing there so abundantly, his family following the slowly moving herd by wagon" (6).

The family eventually settled on a homestead in Idaho, "just across Snake River where that mighty stream divides Idaho from Eastern Oregon. Here he and his fine pioneer wife founded a Christian home that soon became known far and wide to the settlers, the miners and the stockmen of that day as a place of friendliness and hospitality" (6).

This fond, bright family account of Mary Ellen's adult life does not capture the thin edge she lived on. Babies died. Children took terribly ill, just as her sisters had on the trail. John died young, at age forty-five, leaving his widow with the ranch and young children to raise (6). But everything Mary Ellen's own parents had "put" her through, had prepared her to stand up to such troubles. With a love tinged with a firmness hard to imagine today, they had asked her at an incredibly early age to nurse the ill and care for the animals. They gave her the tools she needed to cope with her adult life and she moved through her world with confidence.

Phyllis Lyons, a librarian for the Idaho State Historical Society, and an Applegate descendant, says:

Events of Mary Ellen's life may sound exotic to many, but they were just every day life here. She would have done all of the cooking on a wood stove, raised a garden, and preserved the produce. During the haying season and branding, and when they were shearing the sheep (they had about 1500 sheep and 39 cows with calves) she would have cooked for her own family and all the extra help. She may have bottlefed the bum lambs (orphan lambs). Her laundry would have been done in the yard in a large pot of water heated over an open fire. She would have made her own soap. She would have made the family's clothing. The Applegate family were Baptists and would have attended church often.[5]

After Mary Ellen's husband died, she relied for help on her grown sons and on John's brother Samuel William Applegate, Phyllis' great-great-grandfather. She continued to move on in her life, despite the losses and struggle, and remarried a teacher, Lyell Verbeck, in 1887, who also served as a state representative in the Idaho legislature (ibid.).

Today the Applegate descendants cherish Mary Ellen's story, as well as a breadboard she carved on the trail when she was nine years old. Using a hot poker heated in one of their many campfires, she spelled out "Bread Makes the Butter Fly" in the pine. Rodney Applegate, former chief administrator of the Walla Walla General Hospital in the state of Washington, safekeeps the family heirloom now; a simple relic from a much more rigorous but rich domestic past.[6]

The other four primary characters from the nineteenth century—Lucy Larcom, Harriet Jacobs and her daughter Louisa, and Ethel Spencer—made the radical decision not to marry. Lucy and Ethel, in particular, struggled with how to reconcile their career aspirations (though they would not have used the word "career"), and the demands they would face if they raised families.

After ten years in the Lowell, Massachusetts, mills, Lucy Larcom went to Illinois with her sister Emeline's family. They traveled by train, canal, and boat before settling in their four-room, dirt-floor house thirty miles outside of St. Louis. For years, with the din from the machines as a backdrop, Lucy had plotted her escape. "This was the plan that indefinitely shaped itself in my mind as I returned to my work in the spinning room and which I followed, not without many breaks and hindrances for the next six to seven years, to learn all I could, so that I should be fit to teach or to write, as the way opened."[7]

She had met with some success with her writing already and had sold several poems, including "The Rose Enthroned," to the *Atlantic Monthly*, but the small fees she earned from her work made it clear that only teaching would provide the income she would need to support herself. Western towns desperate for teachers advertised in eastern newspapers and magazines, so Lucy knew she could find work if she went with Emeline and Emeline's husband, George Spaulding.

George's brother Frank also trailed along for a time, wooing Lucy all the while, even as late as 1846, but she was not interested. Her fear of marriage just intensified as she watched her talented, creative older sister get weighed down by eleven children (only four of whom survived) and a dreary day-to-day life out on the prairie. In a letter to a friend, Lucy exclaimed, "Talk to me about getting married and settling down here in the West! I would not do that thing till I'm a greater goose than I am now, for love nor money. It is a common saying here, that 'this is a fine country for men and dogs, but women and oxen have to take it.' The secret of it is that farmer's wives have to do all their work in one room, without help, and almost nothing to work with."[8]

But as a single woman in a time when nearly all jobs paying a livable wage were filled by men, she faced the dilemma of earning a living and being autonomous without being unwomanly. Teaching offered the best way out, but she found it tedious. Attendance could be spotty, especially around harvest time, and books and supplies were lacking. On paper she earned more than she did at the mill, but she often had trouble collecting her wages. A great lover of the outdoors, she did embrace the wildlife and flowers of the prairie, but never developed more than a lukewarm feeling for Illinois and the life she built for herself there.

By 1852, intent on not marrying Frank, and tired of the close quarters of the Spaulding's house, she returned to New England, where she eventually reentered the teaching field at Wheaton Seminary in Norton, Massachusetts. Still feeling less than gratified by her responsibilities, which included living with ten girls, she took great pleasure in being close to Boston again, and the literary circle there headed by her good friend John Greenleaf Whittier.

For the next ten years she published verse in all sorts of magazines and began to establish a national reputation. Eventually, she was able to leave teaching entirely and retreat to a house she bought in her hometown of Beverly, Massachusetts. She kept a niece with her to do all the housekeeping and cooking, because Lucy felt "completely bored by domestic duties that interrupted her writing." Her deep attention to her craft and her popularity with the masses made her a peer among such notables as Harriet Beecher Stowe, Whittier, and Henry Longfellow (2).

Today, we find her hymnlike verses quaint, but they matched the style of the time. In "Fallow," she writes on the issue of God and nature so common in most of her poems.

> Her wild soil you may subdue
> Tortured by hoe and harrow;
> But leave her for a year or two,
> And see: she stands and laughs at you
> with hardhack, mullein, yarrow.
>
> Dear Earth, the world is hard to please:
> Yet heaven's breath gently passes
> Into the lives of flowers like these;
> and I lay down at blessed ease
> Among thy weeds and grasses. (178)

When Lucy died unwed, childless, and relatively poor, many of her generation would have defined her life choice as a failure, but she clearly did not see it as such. She had a calling and had the strength and focus to pursue it. In 1924, on the one-hundredth anniversary of her death, the *Boston Transcript* ran a large feature on her, calling her one of the most notable writer's of her time (2).

Ethel Spencer and Harriet Jacobs and her daughter Louisa also went into teaching, basically the best career available to them at the time. Ethel struggled with her Sunday school curriculum for years; she was a woman with little faith and no patience for church dogma. She escaped by following her sisters to college where she took to literature and writing with a great passion. She graduated from Radcliffe and attended St. Hilda's at Oxford in England. From 1920 to 1955, she taught English at the Carnegie Institute of Technology in Pittsburgh and was head of the General Studies Department when she died.[9]

Nearly all of her siblings, except one sister with weak health, got married and had families. In her memoir about her childhood, Ethel does not explain why she took her less conventional route, but she constantly refers to her mother's strong feelings about education, and may have felt her life followed the track Mrs. Spencer would have pursued herself if she had not had a family.

The fact that the two slave girls—Harriet and Louisa—had careers of any sort is testimony to their astounding strength and talent. When Harriet stowed away on that riverboat after seven years in a garret, she could barely stand. All the years of stillness and silence had ruined her circulation and her voice. The fresh air off the water must have felt almost intimidating with its promise of freedom and openness. She eventually made her way to Boston, where she found a position as a nanny for the Willis family, which provided her employment off and on for decades.

Chased by slave catchers, Harriet had to move in and out of her new life like a shadow. For a time she spent several rare years with both of her children and herself under one roof, but then her son went off with an uncle to California to pan for gold and then to Australia. Harriet never heard from him again.

When Louisa reached young adulthood, Harriet had to face the painful decision of letting her go as well so Louisa could attend a school in New York run by abolitionists.

For two years my daughter and I supported ourselves comfortably in Boston. At the end of that time, my brother William offered to send Louisa to a boarding school. It required great effort for me to consent to part with her, for I had few near ties, and it was her presence that made my two little rooms seem home-like. But my judgment prevailed over my selfish feelings. I made preparations for her departure.[10]

The day Louisa left with her uncle for the school in Clinton, New York, Harriet recalled:

It seemed as if all the sunshine had gone away. My little room was dreadfully lonely. I was thankful when a message came from a lady, accustomed to employ me, requesting me to come and sew in her family for several weeks. On my return, I found a letter from brother [John]. He thought of opening an antislavery reading room in Rochester, and combining that with the sale of some books and stationery; and he wanted me to unite with him. (213)

The year 1849, which was the year Louisa went to school and Harriet headed for Rochester, New York, marked a great turning point for both women. For the first time they broke from the sewing, cleaning, and other domestic chores, which had taken up all of their energies, and turned to a life of education and social work. Harriet stayed in the bookstore less than a year, but while in Rochester she befriended Amy Post, the famous antislavery feminist, who encouraged Harriet to write a book about her life as a slave.

Harriet actually approached Harriet Beecher Stowe with her story but feared that the author would steal her material when Stowe wrote back and suggested the tale be included in *A Key to Uncle Tom's Cabin*. By 1853, Harriet decided to write the book herself.[11] Over the next five years, with some editing help from her newly educated daughter, Harriet scratched away. In her foreword to the book, Amy Post remarks on how Harriet had to "earn her living by her own labor. . . . Several times she has been obliged to leave her employments, in order to fly from the man-hunters and woman-hunters of our land; but she pressed through all of these obstacles and overcame them. After the labors of the day were over, she traced secretly and wearily, by the midnight lamp, a truthful record of her eventful life."[12]

It took some convincing on Post's part to get Harriet to be specific about Dr. Norcom's advances. Harriet feared it would make her look poorly and knew such scandalous tales would offend most Americans. "The burden of these memories lay heavily on her spirit," Post wrote, "I urged her to consent to the publication of her narrative; for I felt that it would arouse people to a more earnest work for the disinthralment of millions still remaining in that soul-crushing condition, which was so unendurable to her."[13]

Of course, as any author can attest, simply writing her book did not guarantee it would be published. In 1858 she actually sailed to England in an effort to sell the rights there, but came back empty-handed. The following year she finally picked up a publisher in Boston, but they promptly went bankrupt. A year later she went through the same cycle with another printer. When the Confederates fired the first shot on Fort Sumter in 1861, Harriet was in Philadelphia buying the plates of her own book and arranging to produce it herself. Published in the United States that year, it appeared in England under the title, *The Deeper Wrong*, in 1862.

After the publication of *Incidents in the Life of a Slave Girl* and the onset of the Civil War, Harriet and Louisa embarked on an astounding cycle of relief work. They went to Alexandria, Virginia, to teach runaway slaves and doled out food and clothing in Washington, D.C., and Savannah, Georgia. Sponsored by a Quaker church, they went to London in 1868 and raised money for an orphanage in Savannah. They came back with 100 pounds sterling, but told their patrons to reconsider building anything in Savannah, a racist town.

For the next few decades mother and daughter worked in tandem, using their rare status as literate black women to help others who had come from the same abusive backgrounds they had escaped. They ran fund-raisers, relief agencies, even a boardinghouse. By the 1870s, both women had settled in Washington, D.C., where Louisa participated in the National Association of Colored Women. Harriet died in 1897, at the age of eighty-four, with her daughter by her side, whom she had freed from the double cross of slavery and illiteracy.

On the overall spectrum of the girls profiled in this book who lived in the eighteenth and nineteenth centuries, Amanda, the German immigrant who worked for the Spencer household in the early 1900s, falls somewhere between the slaves and the career women. Domestic work crowded her early years, as she cooked long hours in the kitchen on Amberson Avenue. Like Harriet and Louisa, no one cared much if she learned how to read and write, but she studied on her own anyway in the quiet, tired hours before bed. Amanda freed herself from the drudgery that faced many immigrant girls, who married factory workers, when she wed Dr. Klein.

Despite her improved circumstances, she remained the frugal immigrant, ever mindful of what a thin line she lived on as a newcomer. In her memoir, Ethel writes:

Once after an evening call, Bertha [another houseworker and friend of Amanda's] reported with disgust that when Mr. Klein did not come home for supper, Amanda put the steak back in the ice box and ate scraps. But this policy must have paid off for the Kleins prospered. Years later, perhaps in the early thirties, Amanda came to our house one day to see Mother. Completely American in appearance and in excellent command of English, she was quite an impressive person, an example of the American success story at its best. One of her sons, she told us, was a doctor, and the other was studying mathematics at Carnegie Institute of Technology. I think Mother felt proud of having helped make so worthy an American citizen as Amanda.[14]

So Amanda may not have been able to follow Ethel into college and beyond, but Amanda's children did. Indeed, Amanda's son studied math at Carnegie during the same years Ethel worked there as an English professor. Bertha's brief account of Amanda's frugal ways hints at a person with goals and an eye on the future.

The girls who grew up in the twentieth century reflect a growing struggle within daughters in general with how to balance their own needs against the demands of their families. Women such as Ethel clearly felt they could not have children and a career, so they made a choice. Connie Sullivan marks the first character in this book who refused to see it as an either/or option and deliberately set out to have both a family and a work life.

Connie wound up in a boot camp in New York State after joining the navy in 1944, where she proved an exceptional recruit. Few of the other girls had come from such large, demanding families. Scrubbing steps and peeling mountains of potatoes made Connie feel right at home. By the end of the eight-week stint, she was chosen to give the marching orders for her platoon and rode the limousine with the officers to the train. "I remember standing there in the sun, barking the command and giving a crisp salute. Boy, that was a great moment!"[15]

Stationed outside Washington, D.C., where she worked as a draftsman making maps for American pilots, the small-town girl from Pawtucket, Rhode Island, and Springfield, Massachusetts, found herself in the middle of one of the hottest cities for young people in the United States. Thousands of servicemen and women descended on the capital, packing the dance halls and clogging the lines to the movie theaters. "You had to stand in line through a full show to get a ticket to the next one," Connie recalls with a laugh. Many of the recruits lived in makeshift barracks along the banks of the Potomac River, but Connie managed to find an apartment to share with three other girls near their offices in Suitland, Maryland.

When the war ended less than twenty-three months later, Petty Officer Sullivan Third Class used the G.I. Bill to pay for her college education at Sargent College (now part of Boston University). She did not have any spare cash for clothes, so "I had to wear my Navy outfit all through school. I did have one evening gown I'd bought with a war bond. I went all over town in that."

Cash and clothes poor, completely reliant on her own resources, Connie made up her mind to graduate with a practical skill and majored in physical therapy. Now age twenty-four, it never occurred to her "that twelve hundred hungry men would be pouring" into the Harvard Law School campus that backed up to Sargent College. "The place was jammed with men wanting to get married. They were all worried that there'd be no girls left. I got a proposal every three weeks!" She refused them all for the first two years, intent on completing college and starting a physical therapy business of her own. But toward the end of her sophomore year, she met and fell in love with James Collins, a penniless Irish Catholic who attended Harvard Law School, who, like her, had used the G.I. Bill to get himself through school. They married in Connie's junior year and had their first child, James, before she graduated, but she went on to complete all her course work. "I'd leave the baby in the hallway while I took class. Other students would come by and check on him and write down if they'd changed his diaper or fed him. He became the class baby."

But after graduation, Connie's balancing act just intensified. She had three more children between 1953 and 1961, which kept her at home for most of those years. Jim decided to make a career in politics, which meant little cash but lots of time-intensive campaigning, first for town council, then for Congress as the Republican candidate from his hometown of Hartford, Connecticut, in 1962 and 1964. Jim never won an election and Connie never opened her own physical therapy practice, but they both thrived on the political life, making friends, discussing issues, and hitting the pavement for votes with children and flyers in hand.

To complement her husband's efforts, Connie joined and eventually became president of the Connecticut Federation of Republican Women. Irate over the lack of credit the women received for all their envelope stuffing and other volunteer work on behalf of the male candidates, Connie insisted they be given an alternate delegate spot to the Republican National Convention. The men refused to concede such a ripe perk, so Connie called for a statewide work stoppage. No flyers folded or handed out. No get-out-the-vote drives. The Republican Party relented immediately. Connie Sullivan Collins ended up winning her battle and took as her prize the alternate delegate seat at the Nixon/Agnew Convention in Miami in 1968. Her successors as president of the Federation have had that seat ever since.

During these busy years when she raised her young children and worked in politics, Connie never lost sight of the fact that she wanted some sort of paying work of her own. She returned to school in the late 1960s and earned a master's degree in education. She taught in the public elementary schools in Hartford for ten years, many of them part time so she could juggle her other interests.

She was ready to quit teaching altogether when her husband died unexpectedly of cancer at the age of fifty-six. All his years of hard work for the Republican Party had netted him a job as a State Supreme Court judge, which left his widow a small pension, but not enough to support a family on. Financially trapped, Connie had to stay in her job.

Unlike Lucy Larcom's mother, who lacked the skills to manage or make money, Connie had the tools she needed to manage precisely because she'd been taught to provide for herself from an early age. "The fact I was one of the oldest in a large family and was expected to do so much—and I *did* it—gave me a sense of accomplishment from an early age," she says. "I watched my parents, the two of them, and the way they struggled to care for nine children, two grandmothers, and a business and I thought, 'If they can do that much I can certainly do what's expected of me.'"

Using her teaching salary as a starting point, Connie got involved in real estate and the stock market and used her gains from those investments to help pay for the college educations of her two youngest daughters. Like her parents, she never doubted she would send them. And despite the exhausting pace, especially in the inner-city classroom she ran, she "had no problem working long hours because I had always worked long hours. I was grateful to have a job and grateful to have a roof over my head and some food. I thanked God for it. My mother and father were on their knees every night praying to God."

Connie was remarried in August 1985 to George Cain, a lawyer from Connecticut. By that time all of her children were educated and on their own. She now lives comfortably in retirement in Farmington, Connecticut.

Lynn Genesko's adult life mirrors Connie's, despite their very different paths, because it reflects a similar level of self-reliance and discipline. Connie learned these skills playing the essential daughter to a large family; Lynn learned them as an Olympic-quality swimmer.

Lynn horrified her parents when she dropped out of the University of Miami and returned home after just one year of college. Burnt out on swimming and into drugs, she drifted for a time. Tensions were high in the Genesko household by the time she moved into an apartment of her own and enrolled at Montclair State University in Upper Montclair, New Jersey. She had to work full time to pay the bills and tuition, so she took classes erratically, but earning an education the hard way proved more fulfilling for her than the free ride and beaches she had been offered in Florida.

When she graduated in 1979, she got involved in designing health clubs for a time, then got back into swimming as a coach. She took over a small YMCA youth team and made it into a powerhouse. "When I finished with them we had 250 athletes, and nine assistant coaches and a national champion, so I think I did a good job for them."[16]

This pattern of taking on a huge project and being self-driven continues to characterize Lynn's life. When her husband, Drew, opened up a comedy club (his second one), they sold lots of objects from the first club to help finance the purchase. "People loved the stuff," she says.

And Lynn's newest project was born. "I figured there was money to be made in buying and selling all of these things." She became a regular at auctions and yard sales and went to school so she could become a certified appraiser. Her whole family is in the business now, including her parents and her husband, who closed down his clubs to join her. "It's so interesting," Lynn says. "You never know what you're going to come across. Right now I'm sitting with a first edition of *Out of Africa* in my lap. So cool."

As a child, her family centered its life around her swimming, often to the detriment of others, especially the middle sister, who remains estranged. But as an adult, they all benefit from Lynn's goals, because its a business that they can each play a part in. "Being an athlete was so vital to whom I became in the end. It taught me so much about being responsible." But she also acknowledges it caused some damaged and put undue strain on her parents in terms of the amount of time and money they had to commit to her. "But I've made it up to all of them since," she adds with a laugh, clearly glad to shoulder the responsibility of being in charge for the sake of the group, not the gold medal, this time around.

Of all of the characters profiled in this book, Beverly Hill struggled the most to find a role for herself both domestically and professionally. Raised in the 1950s, when girls were encouraged to explore little beyond marriage and children, Beverly did not really benefit from having a working mother as a role model, in part because her own parents had so few expectations of her. "My childhood did not prepare me for a damn thing," she says today. "In fact, it slowed me down. I should not have felt so insecure about everything."[17]

It took the helping hand of outsiders to get her on a more focused track. A girlfriend named Mary Lee, who worked as a model, convinced the five foot, one-hundred-pound Beverly to "fluff" herself up and go into dancing.

When you're not attractive and have not come into your own, you're afraid of everything. I was insecure. But this tall girl was gorgeous and she said anyone can be attractive. Then I developed. I had a figure by the time I was twenty-one—better than hers! Once I was a performer that was a real confidence builder. It makes you feel good about yourself, especially if you were an ugly duckling, and that's how I saw myself—as an ugly duckling.

A scout from the Ringling Brothers Circus convinced her to travel with them. They needed trim, athletic girls to do some of the more difficult tricks and more black performers. "I trained in Florida for a time. I was a good athlete. I was only the second black dancer with Ringling Brothers. I had to represent my race in all the towns so I got interviewed a lot. Me and the one black clown."

She became homesick after a few years on the road and returned to Los Angeles, where she continued to dance in nightclubs, but with an eye on something else. "I realized I was getting a bit old for it and had to move on." Another friend told her about the Equal Opportunity Program at the University of Southern California. "Just the sort of program they're getting rid of now," she says, "but I never could have made it without it. If you were poor but smart, they gave you money, and if you were a lousy student but had potential, they gave you a chance."

At the age of thirty-three Beverly tackled college. At first she wanted to major in home economics, but the teachers told her it was a dying field with no future. She turned to what she considered a neutral major, history, and graduated in 1982. With degree in hand, she continued to drift for a while, first working as a secretary and then in accounting. Today, she interviews welfare applicants and helps decide if they should get government aid or not. Her voice falls flat a bit when she says this, but perks up noticeably when she starts talking about her old love: sewing. "I do not do many quilts anymore, but I do a lot of black things. Black items and book covers and Barbie doll clothes. Ooooh, I can make a thousand dollars doing that in no time at all. I still like doing clothes and decorating for people at retirement homes and such."

She says she never married because she thinks most women do it for all the wrong reasons. Sometimes she regrets her decision, primarily for financial reasons. "I realize now that a single woman out here can't have as many material things. I'd like a different house, a different neighborhood. That bothers me."

She did have a child on her own—deliberately—who is now in her twenties and facing the life choices her own mother struggled with when she was a young girl with low self-esteem and no clear vision for who she could be. Beverly feels she did well by Vanessa, and knows she will move more confidently than she did, burdened less by sexism and racism.

Most of the girls profiled in this book grew no taller than five-foot-seven and were petite as young women. Connie, Beverly, Harriet, Louisa, Mollie, Lizzie—all of them barely topped one hundred pounds each. Even Lynn, the world-class athlete, has matured into an average-size woman, whom most people would never pick out as physically strong. Only the sportswoman's swagger that she still retains gives her away—the walk of the sprinter and the risk taker.

Like most people, these girls had to face their adult challenges by using tools from within themselves; not quick feet, or strong hands, but nimble minds and resilient spirits. What sets most of them apart from many of the daughters we see today is that they faced their challenges with such steadiness. The strongest of them—as measured by their firm purpose and bright spirit—came from backgrounds in which they had a clear and vital domestic role within their families. In units in which that role became fuzzy or nonexistent, the girls show a marked decline in confidence.

Daughters had every right to want to free themselves from the drudgeries of hand-washed laundry, dishes, cooking, and child care, but in their attempts to escape, they skipped over learning experiences that provided their predecessors with crucial survival skills. Not just concrete talents such as sewing, which is of little use in the practical sense today, but abstract skills such as discipline, consideration, and self-reliance, which are necessary in any person's lifetime.

Some families, such as the Hodgkins, have turned to sports to fill the gap, but the most astute parents recognize it is not a fair and full exchange. Cindy Hodgkins saw early in her role as parent to three daughters that giving her children the emotional tools for survival was the most important thing she could do. If soccer served that end, fine, but only if it served that end.

Most of the parents behind the girls in this book gave their daughters the tools they needed to survive as adults, even if it meant facing the death of a child and/or a husband or the strain of poverty. Their domestic lives were full enough, demanding enough to produce resilient, self-reliant, courageous offspring. Not enough Americans can make such claims today.

Obviously, many daughters, such as Mary Ellen Todd and Lucy Larcom, were taxed harshly, even abused by today's standards, but they were also loved with a conviction that left little doubt that they were valued. The physical labor they did, mingled with love and appreciation, translated into an emotional well-being that allowed them to face very trying experiences as adults.

We need to become better tool givers to our daughters by borrowing the domestic dynamic of the past, but balancing it with the fairer, less sexist standards we know we should follow today. Chores and child care are not the sole province of women and girls. All children have a right and should be encouraged to aspire to goals that fulfill them personally. But let us give them the emotional strength they will need to follow their aspirations, by putting renewed focus and value on the role they play at home.

NOTES

PREFACE

1. Mary Benn and Debra Edwards, "Adolescent Chores: The Differences between Dual and Single-Earner Families," *Journal of Marriage and Family* 52 (May 1990): 361–513, especially pp. 362–363.

INTRODUCTION

1. Lucy Larcom, *A New England Girlhood* (Houghton Mifflin, 1889), p. 155.

2. See Michaele Weissman and Carol Hymowitz, *A History of Women in America* (Bantam Books, 1978).

3. Ibid.

4. Conrad R. Stein, *The Story of Child Labor Laws* (Children's Press, 1984), 8.

5. See Weissman and Hymowitz, *History*.

6. Barbara Miller Solomon, *In the Company of Educated Women* (Yale University Press, 1985), xvii.

7. Mary Gregory Powell, "Scenes of Childhood," *Fireside Sentinel* (Alexandria [Va.] Historical Collection, 1990), 4(1):6.

8. Weissman and Hymowitz, *History,* 220.

9. T. H. Watkins, *The Great Depression: America in the 1930s* (Little, Brown and Company, 1993), 115.

10. Connie Sullivan, interview with author, Farmington, Conn., February 12, 1999.

11. Joan Jacobs Brumberg, *The Body Project: An Intimate History of American Girls* (Random House, 1997), 18.

12. Mary Pipher, *Reviving Ophelia: Saving the Selves of Adolescent Girls* (Ballantine Books, 1994).

13. Brumberg, *The Body Project*, 6.

14. Lynn Genesko, personal interviews with the author, Woodbridge, New Jersey, October 7, 1999.

SECTION ONE

1. Nicholas Orme, *Medieval Children* (Yale University Press, 2001), 10.

2. See Philippe Aries, *Centuries of Childhood: A Social History of Family Life* (Vintage Books, 1962).

3. See John Warner, *Colonial American Home Life* (Franklin Watts, 1993).

4. Eliza Cabot, *Reminiscences of Mrs. Eliza Cabot* (Schlesinger Library).

5. Solomon, *In the Company of Educated Women*, 2.

6. Edward Boykin, ed., *To the Girls and Boys: Being the Delightful Little Known Letters of Thomas Jefferson to and from his Children and Grandchildren* (Funk and Wagnells, 1964), 66.

7. See Harriet Jacobs, *Incidents in the Life of a Slave Girl* (New American Library, 2000).

8. See Adrietta Applegate Hixon, *On to Oregon* (Ye Galleon Press, 1993).

9. See Powell, "Scenes of Childhood," 4(2).

1797: LIZZIE

1. See the IBoston Web site: neaq.org/beyond/pubs/harbor.history.

2. Ibid.

3. See Howard Brett, *Boston: A Social History* (Hawthorn Books, 1976).

4. See Solomon, *In the Company of Educated Women*.

5. Cabot, *Reminiscences*, 9.

6. Betty Ring, *Girlhood Embroidery: American Samplers and Pictorial Needlework, 1680–1850* (Knopf, 1993), 1:3.

7. Cabot, *Reminiscences*, 20.

8. See Brett, *Boston*.

9. Cabot, *Reminiscences*, 22.

10. Leonard Fisher, *The School Masters* (Franklin Watts, 1967), 32.

11. Hannah More, *Search after Happiness*, microforms, McardII American 1714–1830, Georgetown University.

12. Cabot, *Reminiscences*, 24.

1830–1840: LUCY

1. Brook Hindle and Stevens Lubar, *Engines of Change: The American Industrial Revolution 1790–1860* (Smithsonian Institution Press, 1986), 196.

2. Shirley Marchalonis, *The Worlds of Lucy Larcom, 1824–1893* (University of Georgia Press, 1989), 12.

3. Larcom, *A New England Girlhood*, 88.

4. Marchalonis, *Worlds of Lucy*, 12.

5. Larcom, *A New England Girlhood*, 160.

6. Marchalonis, *Worlds of Lucy*, 23.

7. Larcom, *A New England Girlhood*, 146.

8. Marchalonis, *Worlds of Lucy*, 29.

9. Larcom, *A New England Girlhood*, 153.

10. Marchalonis, *Worlds of Lucy*, 35.

11. Larcom, *A New England Girlhood*, 198.

1852: MARY ELLEN

1. Elliott West, *Growing Up with the Country: Childhood on the Far Western Frontier* (University of Mexico Press, 1989), 12.

2. Adrietta Applegate Hixon, *On to Oregon* (Ye Galleon Press, 1993), 21.

3. *Bible*, Revised Standard Version, Thomas Nelson, Inc., 1971, verses 1–7.

4. Hixon, *On to Oregon*, 101.

ENSLAVED: HARRIET AND LOUISA

1. Wilma King, *Stolen Childhood: Slave Youth in 19th Century America* (Indiana University Press, 1995), 11.

2. Jacobs, *Incidents*, 1.

3. King, *Stolen Childhood*, 11.

4. Jacobs, *Incidents*, 12.

5. See Brumberg, *The Body Project*.

6. Jacobs, *Incidents*, 58–59.

7. King, *Stolen Childhood*, 1.

8. Jacobs, *Incidents*, 109.

9. Bob Tegart, historian in Clinton, New York (btegart@dreamscape.com), personal communication, March 1999.

10. Jacobs, *Incidents* (Harvard University, 1987), 289 n.1.

1861: MOLLIE

1. Census Data, 1860.

2. *World Book Encyclopedia* online.

3. Powell, "Scenes of Childhood," 4:21.

4. Mary Powell, *The History of Old Alexandria VA 1749–1861* (Family Line Publications, 1995), 334.

5. Powell, "Scenes of Childhood," 4:10.

6. William Hurd, *Alexandria, VA 1861–65,* 3rd ed. (Ft. Ward Museum,1989).

7. Powell, "Scenes of Childhood," 4:23.

8. William Hurd and James Barber, *Alexandria History: Beleaguered Alexandria, 1861–1865* (Alexandria [VA] Historical Society, 1982), 8.

9. Powell, "Scenes of Childhood," 4:34.

10. Hurd, *Alexandria,* 10.

11. Powell, "Scenes of Childhood," 4:23.

12. Powell, *History of Old Alexandria,* 156.

13. Powell, "Scenes of Childhood," 4:6.

SECTION TWO

1. Ethel Spencer, *The Spencers of Amberson Avenue: A Turn-of-the-Century Memoir* (University of Pittsburgh Press, 1983), 81–82.

2. Samuel Hays, *City at the Point: Essays on the Social History of Pittsburgh* (University of Pittsburgh Press, 1989), 46.

1900–1914: ETHEL AND AMANDA

1. Spencer, *Spencers,* 8.

2. Kahren Hellerstedt, Joanne Moore, Ellen Rosenthal, and Louise Wells, *The Pittsburgh Home of Henry Clay Frick* (Henry Clay Frick Foundation and the University of Pittsburgh Press, 1988), 12; see also Hays, *City at the Point,* 193.

3. Hays, *City at the Point,* 10.

4. See Thomas Bell, *Out of This Furnace* (University of Pittsburgh Press, 1976).

5. Spencer, *Spencers,* 32–33.

6. Frances Couvares, *The Remaking of Pittsburgh: Class and Culture in an Industrializing City 1877–1919* (State University of New York Press, 1984).

7. Spencer, *Spencers,* 27.

8. Hays, *City at the Point,* 43.

9. Spencer, *Spencers,* 83.

10. Hays, *City at the Point,* 43.

11. Spencer, *Spencers,* 83.

1931–1941: CONNIE

1. Susan Marie Boucher, *The History of Pawtucket, 1635–1986* (Pawtucket, Public Library, 1986), 2, 9, 17, 104.

2. Watkins, *The Great Depression,* 54–55.

3. Ibid., 55; see also Joseph Hawes, *Children between the Wars: American Childhood 1920–1940* (Twayne Publishers and Prentice-Hall, 1997), 104.

4. Ibid.

5. Boucher, *The History of Pawtucket*, 141; also see *Pawtucket, Rhode Island, Statewide History Report* (Rhode Island Historical Preservation Commission, 1978), 33.

6. *Pawtucket, Rhode Island, History Report*, 33.

7. Elizabeth Johnson, *Images of Pawtucket* (Library of Congress, 1979).

8. See Watkins, *The Great Depression*.

9. Boucher, *History of Pawtucket*, 138.

SECTION THREE

1. Annie Dillard, *An American Childhood*, in *Three by Annie Dillard* (HarperPerennial, 1990).

2. Betty Friedan, *The Feminine Mystique* (Dell Publishing, 1962), 15.

3. Betty Friedan, file of personal letters, Carton 19, 679–706 (Schlesinger Library).

1955: BEVERLY AND TINA

1. Wini Breines, *Young, White, and Miserable: Growing Up Female in the Fifties* (Beacon Press, 1992), 50.

2. Tina Hill, telephone interviews with author, Los Angeles, California, January 28, 2000.

3. Sherma Berger Gluck, *Rosie the Riveter Revisited* (Twayne Publishers, 1987), 28.

4. Arthur Verge, *Paradise Transformed: Los Angeles during the Second World War* (Kendall Hunt, 1994), 6.

5. Tina Hill, telephone interview.

6. Gluck, *Rosie*, 49.

7. Beverly Hill, telephone interview with author, Los Angeles, California, June 20, 1999.

8. Tina Hill, telephone interview.

9. Beverly Hill, telephone interview.

10. Friedan, File of letters.

11. Tina Hill, telephone interview.

12. Beverly Hill, telephone interview.

SECTION FOUR

1. Mary Jo Festle, *Playing Nice: Politics and Apologies in Women's Sports* (Columbia University Press, 1996), 166–167.

2. Lynn Genesko, personal interview with the author, Woodbridge, New Jersey, October 7, 1999.

3. Hodgkins family, personal interview with the author, Alexandria, Virginia, November 6, 1999.

1965–1972: LYNN

1. Festle, *Playing Nice*, 224.
2. Lillian and Frank Genesko, personal interview with the author, Woodbridge, New Jersey, October 7, 1999.
3. Lillian Genesko, personal interview.
4. Lynn Genesko, personal interview.
5. Ibid.
6. Francere Sabin, *Women Who Win* (Random House, 1975), 68.
7. Ibid., 68–69.
8. Frank and Lynn Genesko, personal interview.
9. Lynn Genesko, personal interview.
10. Gordon S. White Jr., "15 Scholarships Made Available for Women Athletes by Miami," *New York Times*, 23 May 1973, p. C13.
11. Lillian and Frank Genesko, personal interview.
12. Festle, *Playing Nice*, 224.
13. Lillian and Frank Genesko, personal interview.
14. White, "15 Scholarships."
15. Lillian and Frank Genesko, personal interview.
16. Lillian Genesko, personal interview.
17. Lynn Genesko, personal interview.

2000: MEGGY, ALLY, A.ND SARAH

1. All quotations in this chapter are from my personal interviews with the Hodgkins family, on November 2 and 6, 1999.

CONCLUSION

1. Benn and Edward, "Adolescent Chores," 370.
2. Ibid. Also see Frances Goldscheider and Linda Waite, *New Families, No Families: The Transformation of the American Home* (University of California Press, 1991), 166–167.
3. Ibid., 176.
4. Ibid., 110.
5. Dylan Loeb McCain, "Where is Today's Child? Probably Watching TV," *The New York Times*, 6 December 1999, p. C18.
6. Nancy Signorielli and Margaret Lears, "Children, Television, and Conceptions about Chores," *Sex Roles* 27 (August 1992): 157–170.
7. Jacqueline Salmon, "Kids Seeing More of Mom and Dad," *The Washington Post*, 9 May 2001, p. A1.
8. Jonathan Kaufman, "Domestic Affairs: Even Leftists Have Servants Now," *The Wall Street Journal*, 23 June 1999, p. A1.
9. Benjamin Franklin, "Information for Those Who Would Remove to America," *Norton Anthology of American Literature* (Norton, 1979), 1:275.

10. Henry David Thoreau, *Walden, Norton Anthology of American Literature* (Norton, 1979), 1:1681.

11. Goldscheider and Waite, *New Families, No Families*, 161–162. Also see Erica Gorde, "The Rainbow of Differences in Gays' Children," *The New York Times*, 17 July 2001, p. A1.

12. Goldscheider and Waite, *New Families, No Families*, 161.

13. Elizabeth Austin, "Saving the Home from Martha Stewart," *The Washington Monthly*, December 1999, p. A1.

14. Yvonne Zipp, "Getting Chores Done—From the Sofa," *Christian Science Monitor*, 8 July 1999, p. A1.

15. Austin, "Saving the Home," 12.

EPILOGUE

1. L. Vernon Briggs, *History and Genealogy of the Cabot Family, 1475–1927* (Charles Goodspeed, 1927), 26.

2. Hugh Cabot Collection, Library of Congress, A-99, Section 1, Folder 7.

3. *Alexandria Gazette Packet*, Obituary for Mary Powell, September 27, 1929.

4. Hixon, *On to Oregon*, 6.

5. Phyllis Lyons, librarian at the Idaho State Historical Society, telephone interview with the author, October 23, 1999.

6. Becky Kramer "Bread Board a Reminder of the Oregon Trail," *Walla Walla Union Bulletin*.

7. Larcom, *A New England Girlhood*, 161.

8. Marchalonis, *Worlds of Lucy*, 2.

9. Spencer, *Spencers*, xxxvi.

10. Jacobs, *Incidents* (New American Library), 213.

11. Jacobs, *Incidents* (Harvard), 224.

12. Jacobs, *Incidents* (New American Library), 230.

13. Jacobs, *Incidents* (Harvard), 224–225.

14. Spencer, *Spencers*, 35.

15. Connie Sullivan, personal interview.

16. Lynn Genesko, personal inteview.

17. Beverly Hill, personal interview.

BIBLIOGRAPHY

Alexandria Gazette Packet. Obituary of Mary Powell, September 27, 1929.

Aries, Philippe. *Centuries of Childhood: A Social History of Family Life.* Vintage Books, 1962.

Austin, Elizabeth. "Saving the Home from Martha Stewart." *The Washington Monthly,* December, 1999.

Bell, Thomas. *Out of this Furnace.* University of Pittsburgh Press, 1976.

Benn, Mary, and Debra Edwards. "Adolescent Chores: The Differences between Dual and Single-Earner Families." *Journal of Marriage and Family* 52 (May 1990): 361–513.

Boucher, Susan Marie. *The History of Pawtucket, 1635–1986.* Pawtucket [RI] Public Library, 1986.

Boykin, Edward, ed. *To the Girls and Boys: Being the Delightful Little Known Letters of Thomas Jefferson to and from His Children and Grandchildren.* Funk and Wagnell, 1964.

Breines, Wini. *Young, White, and Miserable: Growing Up Female in the Fifties.* Beacon Press, 1992.

Brett, Howard. *Boston: A Social History.* Hawthorn Books, 1976.

Brumberg, Joan Jacobs. *The Body Project: An Intimate History of American Girls.* Random House, 1997.

Cabot, Eliza. *Reminiscences of Mrs. Eliza Cabot.* Schlesinger Library.

Cabot, Hugh. Hugh Cabot Collection, Library of Congress, A–99, Section 1, Folders 1–7.

Couvares, Frances. *The Remaking of Pittsburgh: Class and Culture in an Industrializing City, 1877–1919.* State University of New York Press, 1984.

Dillard, Annie. *Three by Annie Dillard.* HarperPerennial, 1990.

Festle, Mary Jo. *Playing Nice: Politics and Apologies in Women's Sports*. Columbia University Press, 1996.

Fisher, Leonard. *The School Masters*. Franklin Watts, 1967.

Franklin, Benjamin. "Information to Those Who Would Remove to America." *Norton Anthology of American Literature*, vol. I. Norton, 1979.

Friedan, Betty. *The Feminine Mystique*. Dell Publishing, 1962.

———. File of personal letters, Carton 19, 679–706, Schlesinger Library.

Gluck, Sherma Berger. *Rosie the Riveter Revisited* Twayne Publishers, 1987.

Goldscheider, Frances, and Linda Waite. *New Families, No Families: The Transformation of the American Home*. University of California Press, 1991.

Gorde, Erica. "Rainbow of Differences in Gays' Children." *The New York Times*, 17 July 2001, p. A1.

Green, Harper. *The Uncertainty of Everyday Life: 1915–1945*. HarperCollins, 1992.

Halberstam, David. *The Fifties*. Fawcett Columbine, 1993.

Hawes, Joseph. *Children between the Wars: American Childhood, 1920–1940*. Twayne Publishers and Prentice-Hall, 1997.

Hays, Samuel. *City at the Point: Essays on the Social History of Pittsburgh*. University of Pittsburgh Press, 1989.

Hellerstedt, Kahren, Joanne Moore, Ellen Rosenthal, and Louise Wells. *The Pittsburgh of Henry Clay Frick*. Henry Clay Frick Foundation and the University of Pittsburgh Press, 1988.

Hindle, Brook, and Stevens Lubar. *Engines of Change: The American Industrial Revolution, 1790–1860*. Smithsonian Institution Press, 1986.

Hixon, Adrietta Applegate. *On to Oregon*. Ye Galleon Press, 1993.

Hurd, William. *Alexandria, Virginia 1861–1865*, 3rd ed. Fort Ward Museum, 1989.

Hurd, William, and James Barber. *Alexandria History: Beleaguered Alexandria, 1861–1865*. Alexandria (VA) Historical Society, 1982.

Hutton, Patrick. "Late-Life Historical Reflections of Philippe Aries on the Family in Contemporary Culture." *Journal of Family History* 26 3 (July 2001): 395–410.

IBoston Web site: neaq.org/beyond/pubs.harbor.history.

Jacobs, Harriet. *Incidents in the Life of a Slave Girl.*, ed. Jean Yellin. Harvard University Press, 1987.

———. *Incidents in the Life of a Slave Girl*. New American Library, 2000.

Johnson, Elizabeth. *Images of Pawtucket*. Library of Congress, 1979.

Kaufman, Jonathan. "Domestic Affairs: Even Leftists Have Servants Now." *The Wall Street Journal*, 23 June 1999, p. A1.

King, Wilma. *Stolen Childhood: Slave Youth in 19th Century America*. Indiana University Press, 1995.

Larcom, Lucy. *A New England Girlhood*. Houghton Mifflin, 1889.

Mackoff, Barbara. *Growing a Girl: Seven Strategies for Raising a Strong, Spirited Daughter*. Bantam Doubleday, 1996.

Marchalonis, Shirley. *The Worlds of Lucy Larcom, 1824–1893.* University of Georgia, 1989.

More, Hannah. "Search after Happiness." Microforms, McardII American 1714–1830, Georgetown University.

Orenstein, Peggy. *Young Women, Self-Esteem, and the Confidence Gap.* Anchor Books, 1995.

Orme, Nicholas. *Medieval Children.* Yale University Press, 2001.

Pawtucket, Rhode Island, Statewide History Report. Rhode Island Historical Preservation Commission, 1978.

Pipher, Mary. *Reviving Ophelia: Saving the Selves of Adolescent Girls.* Ballantine Books, 1994.

Powell, Mary. *Fireside Sentinel,* vols. 4–6. Alexandria (VA) Historical Collection, 1990.

———. *The History of Old Alexandria Virginia, 1749–1861.* Family Line Publications, 1995.

Ring, Betty. *Girlhood Embroidery: American Samplers and Pictorial Needlework 1650–1850,* vol. 1. Knopf, 1993.

Sabin, Francere. *Women Who Win.* Random House, 1975.

Salmon, Jacqueline. "Kids Seeing More of Mom and Dad." *The Washington Post,* 9 May 2001, p. A1.

Shorter, Edward. *The Making of the Modern Family.* Basic Books, 1977.

Signorielli, Nancy, and Margaret Lears. "Children, Television, and Conceptions about Chores." *Sex Roles* 27 (August, 1992): 157–70.

Solomon, Barbara Miller. *In the Company of Educated Women.* Yale University Press, 1985.

Spencer, Ethel. *The Spencers of Amberson Avenue: A Turn-of the-Century Memoir.* Ed. Michael P. Weber and Peter N. Stearns. University of Pittsburgh Press, 1983.

Stein, R. Conrad. *The Story of Child Labor Laws.* Children's Press. 1984.

Thoreau, Henry David, *Walden. Norton Anthology of American Literature.* Norton, 1979.

Verge, Arthur. *Paradise Transformed: Los Angeles during the Second World War.* Kendall Hunt, 1994.

Vernon, L. Briggs. *History and Genealogy of the Cabot Family, 1475–1927.* Charles Goodspeed, 1927.

Warner, John. *Colonial American Home Life.* Franklin Watts, 1993.

Watkins, T. H. *The Great Depression: America in the 1930s.* Little, Brown and Company, 1993.

Weissman, Michaele, and Carol Hymowitz. *A History of Women in America.* Bantam Books, 1978.

West, Elliott. *Growing Up with the Country: Childhood on the Far Western Frontier.* University of Mexico Press, 1989.

White, Gordon S. Jr., "Where is Today's Child? Probably Watching TV." *The New York Times,* 6 December, 1999, p. C18.

———. "15 Scholarships Made Available for Women Athletes by Miami." *The New York Times,* 23 May 1973, p. C13.

Zipp, Yvonne. "Getting Chores Done—From the Sofa." *Christian Science Monitor,* 8 July 1999, p. A1.

FURTHER READING

Cott, Nancy. *A Heritage of Her Own: Toward a New Social History of American Women.* Touchstone, 1979.

———, ed. *Roots of Bitterness: Documents of Social History of American Women.* Northeastern University Press, 1986.

Cross, Gary. *Kid's Stuff: Toys and the Changing World of American Girlhood.* Harvard University Press, 1998.

Degler, Carl. *At Odds: Women and the Family from the American Revolution to the Present.* Oxford University Press, 1980.

Formanek-Burnell, Miriam. *Made to Play House: Dolls and the Commercialization of American Girlhood, 1830–1930.* Yale University Press, 1993.

Gershuny, Jonathan, and John Robinson. "Historical Changes in the Household Division of Labor." *Demography* 25(4) (1988): 537–551.

Gilligan, Carol. *Making Connections: The Relational Worlds of Adolescent Girls at Emma Willard School.* Harvard University Press, 1990.

Heron, Liz. *Truth, Dare, or Promise: Growing Up in the Fifties.* Virago, 1985.

Hofferth, Sandra, and John Shandberg. "How American Children Spend Their Time." *Journal of Marriage and Family* 63 (May 2001): 295–308.

Inness, Sherrie, ed. *Delinquents and Debutantes: Twentieth-Century American Girls' Cultures.* New York University Press, 1998.

Jezer, Marty. *The Dark Ages: Life in the United States, 1945–1960.* South End Press, 1982.

Komarovsky, Mirra. *Women in College: Shaping New Feminine Identities.* Basic Books, 1985.

Lasch, Christopher. *Women and the Common Life: Love, Marriage, and Feminism.* Norton, 1998.

Lears, Jackson. *No Place of Grace: Antimodernism and the Transformation of American Culture, 1880–1920.* Pantheon Books, 1981.

Logan, Frances. *All-American Girl: The Ideal of Womanhood in Mid-Nineteenth Century America.* University of Georgia Press, 1989.

Mann, Judith. *The Difference: Growing Up Female in America.* Time-Warner, 1994.

May, Elaine Tyler. *Homeward Bound: American Families in the Cold War Era.* Basic Books, 1989.

Miller, Marlene, ed. *An Intricate Weave: Women Write about Girls and Girlhood.* Iris Editions, 1997.

Mintz, Steve, and Susan Kellogg. *Domestic Revolutions: A Social History of American Family Life.* Dimensions, 1989.

Modell, John. *Into One's Own: From Youth to Adulthood in the U.S., 1920–1975.* University of California Press, 1989.

Nelson, Claudia, and Lynne Vallone, eds. *The Girl's Own: Cultural Histories of the Anglo-American Girl, 1830–1915.* University of Georgia Press, 1994.

Rivers, Caryl. *Beyond Sugar and Spice: How Women Grow, Learn, and Thrive.* Ballantine, 1981.

Rosenberg, Rosalind. *Divided Lives: American Women in the 20th Century.* Hill and Wang, 1992.

Sadker, Myra. *Failing at Fairness: How America's Schools Cheat Girls.* Scribner, 1994.

Sharpe, Sue. *Just Like a Girl: How Girls Learn to Be Women.* Penguin, 1977.

Shorter, Edward. *The Making of the Modern Family.* Basic Books, 1977.

Vallone, Lynne. *Disciplines of Virtue: Girls Culture in the Eighteenth and Nineteenth Centuries.* Yale University Press, 1995.

Walkerdine, Valerie. *Daddy's Girl: Young Girls and Popular Culture.* Harvard University Press, 1997.

INDEX

ABOUT THE AUTHOR

MARY COLLINS is a freelance writer and researcher. She teaches non-fiction writing in the master's degree program at Johns Hopkins University. She has worked as a freelance writer and editor for *National Geographic*, the Smithsonian, and Time-Life Books for the past twelve years.